KINGDOM LESSONS
from
The Fabric of Life

Dear Trudy,

May God fill your life with His joy, peace and hope —

Romans 15:13

Love,

Eunice

EUNICE PORTER

PRESS

TABLE OF CONTENTS

Acknowledgments V
Preface Vii
Dedication Ix
1   WHAT'S IN A NAME?. 11
2   DO YOU KNOW WHO YOU ARE? 13
3   "I'S SAFETY" 15
4   THE CHOPPER 17
5   WHY-NING 19
6   ELLA MAY. 21
7   "AS IT IS IN HEAVEN" 23
8   LEATHER SUITS. 25
9   PETER'S CHOICES. 27
10   THE TIE THAT BINDS 29
11   OOPS!. 31
12   PIGSTY TO PLAYHOUSE 33
13   'DADDY!'. 35
14   RUNAWAY!. 37
15   SUFFERING IN SILENCE 39
16   THAT MISSING PIECE 41
17   KNOTS. 43
18   I CAN SEE! I CAN SEE! 45
19   A NEW FLAVOR 47
20   THORNS 49
21   PIE CRUST. 51
22   NONCONFORMIST. 53
23   CONNECTIONS. 55
24   LEAVING THE NEST 57

# 25	~~T.B.~~	61
# 26	ARTISTS	61
# 27	LEAVES	63
# 28	FIRE!	65
# 29	FLYING	67
# 30	FISHING	69
# 31	THE CALL	71
# 32	LOSING CONTROL	73
# 33	THE LAND OF EUCALYPTUS	75
# 34	CLIMBING	77
# 35	HEE HAW, HEE HAW	79
# 36	CLAY POTS	81
# 37	THE ALUM SOLUTION	83
# 38	WARP AND WEFT	85
# 39	GUNSMOKE	87
# 40	UNCAPPED SPRINGS	89
# 41	MULES	91
# 42	THE WICKED FLEA	93
# 43	THE VANISHING CABBAGE	95
# 44	MALARIA MENACE	97
# 45	THE FOURTH PLAGUE	99
# 46	MARCHING ONE BY ONE	101
# 47	HIDDEN DESTROYERS	103
# 48	A MENAGERIE	105
# 49	MIDNIGHT VISITOR	107
# 50	ON THE HEIGHTS	109
# 51	STAINS OF REBELLION	111
# 52	THE GRACE EXCHANGE	113
# 53	ADOPTED	115
# 54	THE FABRIC SHOP	117
# 55	TIE-DYED TEES	119
# 56	RELINQUISHING	121
# 57	NEW HORIZONS	123
# 58	TRAFFIC TICKET!	125
# 59	CURB CRUNCH	127
# 60	GET DOWN!	129
# 61	A TANGLED WEB	131
# 62	PATCHWORK QUILTS	133

63   FABRICATION 135
64   ABOUT SPROUTS 137
65   OUCH!! 139
66   SPROUTS AGAIN?? 141
67   SKATEBOARDING 143
68   CRUISING DOWN THE RIVER 145
69   A NEW PERSPECTIVE 147
70   CATARACTS 149
71   THE "C" WORD 151
72   LIFE IN THE BLOOD 153
73   VERTIGO 155
74   A DRY AND THIRSTY LAND 157
75   WITCHCRAFT 159
76   I'M SCARED! 161
77   FALLING OR FLYING? 163
78   THE PSYCH WARD 165
79   TELLING A STORY 167
80   THE FAMILY TREE 169
81   BROKEN CONNECTIONS 171
82   WATCH YOUR STEP! 173
83   TEN-POINT LANDING 175
84   GETTING OFF TRACK 177
85   BRUISES 179
86   "LITTLE MISS PIGGY" 181
87   ADDICTED! 183
88   ONE THING LEADS TO ANOTHER 185
89   "THE RAINS CAME DOWN" 187
90   BREAKING SOUL-TIES 189
91   DON'T TOUCH! 191
92   RE-GENERATION 193
93   DNA 195
94   "BEFORE YOU CALL.... 197
95   CHANGING THE FILTER 199
96   100 % PURE 201
97   HANDLE WITH CARE 203
98   "IF YOU LOVE ME" 205
99   GET ON BOARD 207
100   RECAPITULATION 209

ACKNOWLEDGMENTS

Bless you, Reagan McLean, for offering to design my book cover! Thank you for the hours you spent doing the embroidery, which gives it that homespun look, so fitting for the theme and tenor of this book. I appreciate your artistic ability and also your patience in getting it press-ready to the satisfaction of all concerned. I love it, and am <u>so</u> grateful to you!

Bless you, Margie Analise, for volunteering your expertise to set up and design my website–www.euniceporter.com – a special gift to me who am quite illiterate in that field! Thank you, dear friend, for navigating these waters with me and for me! The website is beautiful, and so are you! Thank you for blessing me with your talents!

PREFACE

When I wrote my first book, "He Brought Me Out!", it was designed as a Bible study, based on the truths of Psalm 40:2-3, which in a few words describes our life journey "from the pit to the promised land". My reason for writing it was because for years I seemed to be wandering in the wilderness, not enjoying the blessings and bounty of the abundant life Jesus promised. At a time of extreme spiritual dryness and apathy, I was jolted out of my pitiful situation through a new look at the eternal truths of God's Word. I believe God wanted me to share what He was teaching me, and how life-changing it was.

Some of my friends were expecting that book to be more of an autobiography, a story of my life. Looking back, I suppose my life was fairly interesting, if not exciting. But I never felt it was worth writing a book about. After all, I don't even journal! So, when God began nudging me to write my story—the good, the bad and the ugly, it took me a long time to move forward with it. Then He showed me that He could use the incidents of my life to teach Spiritual truths. Often, He would bring a story to my memory before I had any clue what the lesson was!

This book, specifically designed as devotional readings, is what has come out of the bits of material and interwoven threads that have formed the fabric of my life. It is not my desire to perpetuate my existence through the pages of a book. What I hope and pray is not that you remember the stories, or even learn from my foolish mistakes, but that you will let the lesson from the Word speak to your heart and change your life as it has changed mine. It is only God's Word, by His Spirit, that can do that! Ask Him to work out His truth in your daily life! If you can, find and read the scripture references with each chapter.

Unlike most devotional books, this one does not have a lesson for each day of the year. It is not intended to take the place of your Bible reading/study. You can leave it on your coffee table and pick it up at random, or take it with you on a trip, or on your bus ride to work. You will laugh at some stories, shake your head at others, and perhaps be shocked at some. But do be encouraged that God loves even the strangest and wildest of us, and wants to have sweet, lasting fellowship with us.

May God bless all of you who read these pages!

DEDICATION

I lovingly dedicate this book, first of all to my parents, James <u>Ernest</u> and Ruby Elma (McGhie) Porter for the sacrificial love, care, provision and support you invested in my life, and for the example you were of fidelity, along with strong Christian faith and values. Thank you for your part in giving me a good heritage!

Secondly, to each one of my siblings, whom I appreciate for your uniqueness, for the memories of good times together, for the laughter and sharing, and for helping to shape me into the person I am today. I hope you will forgive me for mentioning your names in print, but this book would not be what it is without you—you are woven into the fabric of my life!

Arla Elizabeth > James <u>Harvey</u> > David Wilfred
Amy Margaret > (Eunice Irene) > Russel John
Mary Elaine > Francis William > Norman Elgin/Pat
Ella May > Albert Ernest > Roy Mervin
Lorna Merle > Lloyd Andrew

Thirdly, to the many friends who have encouraged me along the way, too numerous to count, so special. God bless you all!

KINGDOM LESSONS

from

The Fabric of Life

1
WHAT'S IN A NAME?

I arrived on the scene towards the end of The Great Depression (known as the Dirty Thirties because of the dust storms). It began on October 29, 1929 with the crash of the stock market, and continued until the beginning of World War II on September 3, 1939. I must have sensed that things were pretty bleak out there—with drought, unemployment and food shortages—so I stayed put, building up my reserves of fat until I weighed a whopping ten pounds, twelve ounces (almost five kilograms!) My poor mother! I was the fifth of fourteen she bore, and the last one tipped the scale at eleven pounds! She should have received several medals!

As I grew older, I was amazed that there was always food on the table, clothes on our backs and shelter from the elements; but as a child I took those things for granted, and knew nothing of the hardships faced by my parents and others. It probably helped that we were still on the farm, but I don't remember hearing any stories of lack or loss. No doubt God was watching over us!

In our family we each have two given names—no more, no fewer. Having a United Kingdom heritage, how did I get two Greek names? Eunice, the Biblical name of Timothy's mother, is made up of two words. 'Eu' means good, as in euphoria or utopia; while 'nice' (pronounced *nee' kay*) means victory or victorious (like the Nike sportswear 'V' logo). My other name,

Irene, is the Greek word for peace, which naturally follows a good victory! The question is: Do I live up to my name?

In the Jewish culture, prophetic names are often given to children, to help shape their destiny. Sometimes in the Bible, a person's name is changed by God. When God promised Abram and Sarai a son, He changed both their names to show what He was going to do through them (Gen.17:5-6, 15-16). After Jacob wrestled with God, he was given the name *Israel*, (Prince with God) (Gen.32:27-29). And Jesus gave the unstable Simon the new name *Peter* (rock), on his confession that He was the Christ, the Son of the living God (Matt.16:16-18).

I think one the most wonderful verses in the Bible is John 10:3-4, referring to Jesus, our Good Shepherd: "The sheep hear His voice; and He calls His own sheep by name and leads them out." It really doesn't matter what my name is. What is important is that *I know His voice* and He knows my name! Hallelujah!

2
DO YOU KNOW WHO YOU ARE?

The name Eunice seemed especially difficult for my younger brothers to pronounce, as they began learning to talk. So, a couple of them, who were quite close in age to each other called me 'Ooty'; and to Russel, next in line to me, I was 'Noosis'. Sometimes I still get called one or the other, just for old times' sake. One day a neighbor of ours was doing some handyman work around our farm, and Russel wanted to be where the action was, so kept getting in his way. Finally, in exasperation, he said to Russel, "Do you know you're a nuisance?" Russel, quite insulted, emphatically corrected him with, "I *not* Noosis! I Wussel! He didn't know how to say his name yet, but *he knew who he was*!

A baby isn't very old before he begins to respond to the sound of his name. At the same time, he knows <u>whose</u> he is, learning the sound and sight of his parents and siblings. And, in a normal and healthy environment, it isn't that long before he realizes he is a person in his own right, with his very own identity—not just somebody's brother, or someone's son. He's more than a cog in a wheel. He might actually be a big wheel! Sadly, there are many people of all ages who have lost their identity through rejection, abandonment, abuse, or a co-dependent relationship. They have no sense of self-worth, and blame themselves for past hurts.

The loss of identity brings insecurity, inner conflict, driven-ness, fear, guilt, self-hatred, and other similar negative expressions. In turn these can cause depression, Alzheimer's, lupus, fibromyalgia and Crohn's disease, etc. The problem is compounded because our disease then becomes our identity. So, are we condemned to this, or can we take back our identity and also our health? John 10:10 tells us these have been stolen from us by Satan, the enemy of our souls; but Jesus came to give us abundant life.

If you are a child of God, through faith in Christ, you have been re-born into the Kingdom of God, and are no longer living under Satan's jurisdiction (John 3:3; Col.1:13). It is time to reject the lies of the old kingdom, that say you are worth-less and condemned to a miserable life. It is the truth of the new kingdom that will set you free to be the person God created you to be. Start by forgiving all who have ever hurt you, blessing them rather than cursing them (Jesus' words in Matt.6:14-15; 5:44). Repent of un-forgiveness, bitterness, anger, hatred and anything that is not of God, and renounce them (Eph.4:31-32; Rom.13:12-14).

<u>You have a new identity in Christ</u>. Read the Bible, asking the Holy Spirit to show you who you are. Here are some truths to begin with: Eph.1:3-14, 2:4-10; 3:16-20; Col.1:9-14; 3:1-10; Rom.8:11, 15-17, 31-39; Phil.4:13; 2 Tim.1:7; Heb.4:16; 1 John 3:1; 5:18-20; 1 Cor.6:19-20. <u>This is who you are!</u> Believe it and Live it!!

3
"I'S SAFETY"

*R*ecently, God brought to my remembrance an incident from my early childhood that I don't remember, but that was often retold by my mother. Some of the details I write here may not be exactly as happened, but no matter. I was about three at the time, and was playing a game of Hide-and-Seek with my older siblings. It seems I came out of hiding, and either ran 'home', or perhaps to my father. At any rate I was sure I was safe. So when the person who was 'seeking' ran up and tagged me, I was quite indignant. Using all the vehemence I could muster and express with my relatively tiny size and voice, I addressed my 'tagger' in the best baby-talk I knew: "Don't you *wee-lee-ize* I's safety?"

I smile, as I think about what I have been learning over the past few years in regards to the authority we as Christ-followers have over Satan, the enemy of our souls. Eph.6:12 makes it clear that our war is not against people, but "against spiritual hosts of wickedness in the heavenlies." In 1 Pet.5:8-9 we are told "Your adversary the devil walks about like a roaring lion, seeking whom he may devour. Resist him, steadfast in the faith." Jas.4:7 reinforces this: "Resist the devil, and he will flee from you." And Eph.4:27 says "(*Don't*) give place to the devil"!

The devil/Satan is really God's enemy, and he tries in whatever way he can to destroy God's children. He tempts us to sin by making it look appealing; to doubt God's word; to trust people more than we trust God. He fills us with lies about ourselves, about God and about himself. One of his most effective tactics is to make us believe he doesn't exist at all. He wants us to be in his control, without us even knowing it, so that we berate ourselves for the thoughts we think, and for our out-bursts of anger and hatred; and we don't know how to deal with them.

There are some very effective ways to rout this enemy — and ignoring him isn't one of them! We do not need to fear him, because he was defeated at the cross. He only has power in us as we let him in the door. But we need to resist him. How??

- Know, believe and obey God and His truth (Jas.4:7)
- Draw near to God, with a pure heart (Jas.4:8)
- Wear the armor God has provided for us (Eph.6:10-18)

With all this in place, we need to know that Jesus gave His church authority in His Name to cast out demons (Satan's army of cohorts). See Matt.10:1, 8; Luke 10:17-19; Mark 16:17-18. With all the authority of the name of Jesus, we can say to the evil spirits, "Don't you realize I am safe from your attacks? You have no right to touch me. I am off limits. I am God's child and refuse to be deceived by your lies. Go from me in the name of Jesus of Nazareth!!" Jesus died to set you free. Take back your freedom!

#4
THE CHOPPER

I wasn't very old when my brother, Russel, fourteen months younger, came screaming and crying into the house, obviously in great pain and distress. As my mother rushed to see what was wrong, she wasn't quite prepared for what met her eyes. Russel's big toe was almost severed, hanging pathetically in the midst of the blood that flowed profusely from the wound. Immediately my mother jumped into action, putting the toe back into place and binding it with a bandage. I don't remember the details, but we were miles from a doctor, and had no means of reaching one, so it wasn't an option. I do know my brother's toe reconnected, and healed. At the time, when Russel was asked what he cut it with, he said "the chopper".

No doubt Russel had many times watched his Daddy wield the axe to chop wood for our kitchen stove. Was he trying to help, or was he imitating his father? Maybe both. I think he learned that day that much as he emulated his daddy, he was not quite ready to fill his shoes. I have always been touched by stories of little boys trying to walk in their father's footsteps, wanting to be close to them and watch them work, wanting to help and learn from them, trying to please them and be like them!

No doubt there are many fathers who are not good examples for their children to follow. Some fathers are totally absent from their children's lives, for whatever reason. A good father, who is there for his wife and children as the God-ordained head of the home, brings security and love. He earns their respect. Children are much more willing to obey in this scenario, and usually grow up to be good citizens and good parents themselves.

Eph.5:1-2 exhorts us to "<u>be imitators of God as dear children and walk in love</u>". One of the reasons Jesus came to earth as a man was to show us the Father. He wanted us to know that God the Father is <u>our</u> Father, as we accept His Son as our Savior. Jesus was always obedient to the Father, and did nothing He did not see His Father doing (John 5:30). His Father loved Him with a perfect love, and He loves us the same! (John 17:23) Jesus wants us to know the Father's love, and that this love is in us just as Christ is in us. As we walk in His love we are imitators of Him in glad obedience (John 17:26; 16:27; 14:15, 23).

Let's ponder Jesus' prayer for us before He went to the cross: "that they all may be one, as You, Father, are in Me, and I in You; that they also may be one in Us . . . I in them, and You in Me; that they may be made perfect in one, and that the world may know that You have sent Me, and have loved them as You have loved Me" (John 17:21-23). "<u>Walk just as He walked</u>" (1 John 1:5-6)

5
WHY-NING

I don't remember that whining was a part of life in our home. It might have been tried, but was probably nipped in the bud, so we knew it wasn't tolerated. What I do know, is that when it was time for my sister, at six and a half years of age, to start school, I apparently was inconsolable at the thought of losing my constant playmate to this new adventure, which I was being denied! The rules weren't so strict back then, and my sobbing (or wailing) got me enrolled in Grade One at the age of five, to my delight, and my sister's chagrin. She was stuck with me for the next fifteen years, through high school, and then Bible school. (I suppose I was one of those strong-willed children they talk about today.)

Nobody likes whiners, no matter what age they are. Whining might be excused in a child, but is intolerable in adults. Sadly, God's people are often guilty of this, especially when you look at some synonyms of the word 'whine': fuss, gripe, grouse, bellyache, grumble, and complain. Listen to Israel after they were rescued from slavery in Egypt. "Why did you bring us out to die here in the desert?" "Why do we have to eat this boring manna every day?" "Why do we have to listen to you, Moses?" "Why can't we have a king like other nations, and worship their gods?"

Now listen to yourself, and people around you: "Why did God let this happen to me?" "Why doesn't God give me what I ask for?" "Why did God make me this way?" "Why should I forgive that man who abused me?" "Why do I have to obey the traffic rules?" It seems to me that asking all these <u>why</u> questions is a good indication of the rebellion in our hearts.

If we examine the history of Israel as recorded in the Old Testament, we see that things went much better for them when they obeyed God, and were thankful for His blessings, rather than when they murmured and complained about their miserable circumstances. Maybe our propensity to focus on negative things in our lives just brings us more negative stuff. It really *does* make a difference in our satisfaction level when we "Rejoice always; pray without ceasing; in everything give thanks; for this is the will of God in Christ Jesus for you." (1 Thes.5:16-18) Do you suppose the quenching of the Spirit in the next verse might be connected to a lack of thanksgiving?

Next time you are tempted to complain, take a look at all the things Paul had to complain about (2 Cor. 11:23-28), and yet the message of pure joy that shines through, in the book of Philippians. Here are a few of his words to us: "Do all things without complaining" (2:14); "Be anxious for nothing, but...with thanksgiving, let your requests be made known to God"(4:6); "Rejoice in the Lord always. Again I say, rejoice!" (4:4) Also see 1 Tim.6:6-8 and Heb.13:5.

6
ELLA MAY

I was six years old at the time. My parents had been away for days, and had taken my baby sister with them. My aunt had come to look after my eight siblings and me, and life went on. I think I was at school when Daddy and Momma came home, and I could hardly wait to see them. I was especially excited about seeing my adorable ten-month old sister again.

I will never forget that day, when Daddy picked me up in his arms and carried me into his office. He walked over to a table, and we looked down into a satin-lined wooden box. There was Ella May, so sweet and peaceful 'in sleep', wearing a silky white dress, and clutching a tiny pink flower in her hand, over her heart. I smiled, thinking she had never looked more beautiful. I turned my face to share my joy with Daddy, but he wasn't happy. Why did he look so sad? I was confused, but said nothing, as we left the room; and I was left to wonder what was happening.

On Saturday afternoon, friends and neighbors started to arrive at our home, and there was soon a crowd seated like in church; hymns were sung, and words spoken. Once again I was puzzled, especially at the sight of my ten year old brother convulsed in tears. What did it all mean?

The following Monday, at school, my friend who was a year older and much more worldly-wise than I, accosted me with the words "Eunice, shame on you! You didn't cry *once* at your own sister's funeral!" Her words stung, and I burst into tears at the rebuke. It wasn't until later that it all made sense, when Ella May didn't come back, and Momma was so sad. She and Daddy had watched their precious darling succumb to infantile paralysis (polio) and pneumonia. It must have been devastating, and I am grieving with them as I write today, decades later.

In my innocence I didn't understand such crippling grief, but I know I missed my baby sister. My grief for that loss in my life lay buried for many years, but burst forth in a flood of tears when I was reminded that I probably needed to express my grief, so that God could turn it into joy (Isa.61:1-3; Jer.31:13; 1 Thes.4:13-14). We need to grieve, but we also need to let God comfort us and heal the wounds. Inordinate, sustained grief has a devastating effect in our lives and on our families, because it turns into self-pity, bitterness and depression. This is not what we want or need to carry. Jesus bore our grief, so we could be free from its burden. "Surely He has borne our griefs and carried our sorrows; . . . The chastisement for our peace was upon Him, and by His stripes we are healed" (Isa.53:4-5). He calls out to you in your deep grief today, "Come to Me, all you who labor and are heavy laden, and I will give you rest" (Matt.11:28). Friend, trade in your grief and sorrow today for His abiding joy and peace!

#7
"AS IT IS IN HEAVEN"

In the olden days, when I was young, reciting "The Lord's Prayer" at the beginning of the school day was as much a part of learning as was arithmetic. It wasn't discussed or debated; we just prayed it with bowed heads and closed eyes. You cannot say the same ten lines two hundred times a year without catching at least part of what they mean. Maybe we didn't express it, but we knew there's a heaven and we have a Father there. His name is to be hallowed (What does that *mean?*); and we said He should let things be done on earth like they are in heaven (But, what is *done* in heaven?) We told Him to give us our daily bread, and forgive our *trespasses* (Is that the bad things we do?) Then we say we forgive (This is confusing!) Well, you get my drift. . .

To most children across the country, these were just a series of memorized words in a strange language. Who talks like that? Today, for thousands of grown-up children who recite those same words every week, has much changed? Are these words meaningful and powerful, or senseless gobbledygook said in a mindless sing-song chant? What was Jesus teaching us when He said we should pray like that? Are there some imbedded truths in these words, which need to be mined out and put to use?

Let's briefly explore the words "Your kingdom come. Your will be done on earth as it is in heaven". The two sentences basically say the same thing. In a very real sense, God's kingdom *has* come, and increases every day as people bow the knee to His Lordship, and He sets up His kingdom in their hearts. Out of Jesus' mouth came the words "Indeed, **the kingdom of God is within you**" (Luke 17:20-21). And where His kingdom is, His will is done!

Jesus came to this earth to introduce God's kingdom. Over and over He said "The kingdom of God is near!" Acts 10:38 says "God anointed Jesus of Nazareth with the Holy Spirit and with power, who went about doing good and healing all who were oppressed by the devil, for God was with Him." This, dear friend, is what God's will done on earth looks like. It is not God's will for His people to be sick and oppressed by the devil. Jesus came to *destroy* the works of the devil (1 John 3:8).

The same Spirit who was in Jesus, is within us, to give us the power to do God's will and work on earth (Rom.8:11; Acts 1:8). When God's people are anointed and filled with the Holy Spirit, God's will is being done on earth as it is in heaven. He has given us the authority of His kingdom, to preach the Gospel, heal the sick and cast out evil spirits in Jesus' name (Luke 9:1-2; 10:9, 19; 12:32; Mark 16:15-18; Acts 8:4-8). <u>This is His will, to be done on earth by you and me! Let's get on with Kingdom business!</u>

8
LEATHER SUITS

*D*uring the biting cold Saskatchewan winters, our family would travel to church in a large, horse-drawn sleigh. The younger of us children huddled together on hay in the bed of the sleigh among a few heated stones, snug beneath layers of robes made from the hides of horses (complete with the hair). They were heavy on our small frames, but they protected us from the wind and cold, and I was grateful for them. As you can see, we were pretty dependent on those mostly gentle, faithful horse friends.

Did you know that the first completely adequate and modest suits of clothing, were made by God, for the first couple, Adam and Eve? They were about to leave their beautiful home in the Garden of Eden after their disobedience in eating the forbidden fruit. The clothing they had made when they suddenly realized they were naked, wasn't satisfactory to cover them, so Instead of withering fig leaves, God chose something that would protect them in their new environment, and would last for a good long time as well. Details in the Genesis account are sketchy, but we know that these suits were made of leather! We don't know what they were like, but they were fashioned by the Master Designer who created the earth and sky, the birds and flowers!

In order for Adam and Eve's nakedness to be clothed, God had to slay some of the very animals they had named and tended in the Garden. Did this guilty pair look on as the blood of these animals was spilled in order that they could be clothed? What was going through their minds? I believe there was more involved here than outfitting a couple of people. I can imagine that as God worked, He was teaching them. By now they knew they had sinned against their Creator and dear Friend, and would suffer the consequences–a difficult and sorrowful existence in a cruel world. Was God saying the words He later gave to Moses, "The life of the flesh is in the blood, and I have given it to you upon the altar to make atonement for your souls; for it is the blood that makes atonement for the soul."? (Lev.17:11) Similar words were written later in Heb.9:22, "Without shedding of blood there is no *remission*" i.e. forgiveness.

God knew that one day His own spotless Son would give Himself as a sacrifice on the altar (the cross), and that His blood would purify us from sin, cleansing our conscience from dead works, and redeeming us from all transgressions. The blood of all the animal sacrifices ever shed could only cover sin over, until this Perfect Sacrifice would provide us with His own righteousness in place of all our sin and iniquity (Heb.9:11-15). Praise be to God for His amazing plan of Redemption and Salvation!

#9
PETER'S CHOICES

One of the constants in my early childhood was Peter, a big black cat. I must admit he wasn't a close friend of mine, only because he was an animal, and I tried to steer clear of critters (as much as I could, living on a farm). Peter was really quite friendly, unless he was hungry. Then an unfortunate mouse might find him aggressive and hostile. I preferred cats to mice, so I was okay with him keeping the mouse population under control, as long as I wasn't around to watch the carnage. Peter actually got along with most people, and also the dogs that came and went. My Dad wondered if he was just a bit too friendly, though, when early one morning he saw Peter walking along a path through a field, behind a skunk—one of those cute black and white cat-size creatures that can spray a most obnoxious-smelling fluid on whatever man or beast might pose a threat to him. I'm sure Peter just wanted to make a new friend, and maybe he did, as he returned home later smelling quite normal.

Peter would come into the house in the evening, especially in the cold winter. He loved to curl up by the stove to keep warm. Before bed, Dad would stoke up the fire, and open the oven door to let more heat out into the house. In the morning, he would shut the oven door and stir up the embers, adding wood to heat the house before the family had to get up. One day, as the wood caught fire and the heat started to warm the stove, there was suddenly a loud meowing sound coming from inside the oven. Dad opened the oven door, and Peter, miffed at the indignity, but apparently unharmed, beat an embarrassed retreat.

Sometimes the choices we make may seem benign, but can be potentially dangerous. Out of a sense of loneliness, or wanting to be accepted, we seek friendships with the 'in' crowd, which might bring hurtful, hostile rejection, or lead into a harmful and destructive way of living. Sparrows who try to hobnob with hawks don't fare too well; just so, as the Bible warns, "Evil company corrupts good habits" (1 Cor.15:33); and "My son, if sinners entice you, do not consent" (Prov.1:10).

Just as a warm oven is to a cat, what may seem good at first might lead to disaster. "There is a way that seems right to a man, but its end is the way of death" (Prov.14:12). How can we make choices that are pleasing to God, and will not bring us to destruction? Psa.119 has some excellent answers. "Your word I have hidden in my heart, that I might not sin against You" (v.11); "Through Your precepts I get understanding; therefore I hate every false way" (v.104); "Your word is a lamp to my feet and a light to my path" (v.105); "Direct my steps by Your word, and let no iniquity have dominion over me" (v.133).

#10
THE TIE THAT BINDS

*A*s with many children, it was a momentous occasion for me when I conquered the fine art of tying my shoes. It was a sign of becoming more independent and capable. (As I write this, in an era of slip-on shoes and Velcro fasteners, this feat may be becoming a lost art, along with others replaced by technology). By the way, did you know that the ends of a shoe lace are gathered neatly and wrapped in a small plastic or metal sheath called an aglet? This keeps the lace from unraveling, thus making it easier to thread through the eyelets to lace the shoes up. (Lacing is an art in itself, with room for individual creativity).

A good 'tie' needs to be tight enough to stay in place in the midst of all the foot motions. This prevents the agonizing experience of having to stop in the middle of a race or game to re-tie a shoe! At the same time, it should come untied easily when one of the ends is tugged, without forming a knot, which is quite annoying! As I said, it's an art, designed to keep your feet firmly supported, so they can do what they were meant to do, without pain, strain, danger or embarrassment. The best-fitting lace-up shoe or skate can be harmful to your foot or to other parts of your body, if the laces are loose, causing the foot to wobble; or if dangling laces cause you to trip and fall. A word to the wise!

I am reminded of the words of an old hymn, "Blest be the tie that binds our hearts in Christian love." A more recent one is a prayer for God to "Bind us together in love". These words refer to Col.3:14, where we are admonished to "Put on love, which is the bond of perfection", and to Eph.4:3 – "Keep <u>the unity of the Spirit</u> in the bond of peace." The tie that binds us together is <u>not</u> our doctrine or our denomination. God has placed His Spirit of love and peace in our hearts to "knit *us* together in love" (Rom.5:5; Col.2:2). As the fruit of the Spirit grows in us, and as He distributes His gifts to us, we work together in unity to support the body for the good of all. (See 1 Cor.12:4-11) Think about it!!

To mix metaphors, have you ever typed or written a word that didn't come out quite right because a couple of the letters were switched? '<u>United</u>' can become '<u>untied</u>' if 'I' is misplaced. The love chapter, 1 Cor.13, so clearly describes how the unifying property of love is destroyed by our selfishness, pride and envy. When I am out of line in my attitudes and behavior, how quickly the cords of love can unravel. The body of believers becomes vulnerable, people are hurt and the name of Christ is dishonored.

The shoes of "the preparation of the Gospel of peace" are laced up and tied with love by the Holy Spirit, so that as bearers of the Good News, we will be known by all as disciples of Jesus, because of our "love for one another" (Eph.6:15; John 13:35).

11
OOPS!

t sat in its regal beauty on the washstand in our bedroom at the farm. I don't know how long it had been there. Maybe it had belonged to Grandma, finding its way to our house after her funeral. It would be an antique now, and highly treasured—a basin and pitcher set, delicately crafted (probably in England) from fine china, and tastefully painted with flowers. I am not able to describe it in detail, because I was too young to remember, and alas, its 'life' was cut short, complements of yours truly.

It wasn't intentional, of course. Truthfully, I guess I wasn't the only one to blame, as I have to implicate my sister in the crime. She was older than I, so I suppose, like Adam, I could shift the blame onto her. But she is not here to defend herself, and after all, this is a book of *my* stories. So, I will take full responsibility.

We were being obedient at the time, not running around wildly, jumping on the bed, or throwing things. Our daily chores included making the beds in the morning. As we proceeded, we pulled the big comforter off the bed, and laid it on the wash-stand. We were probably quite careful not to knock over the pitcher-basin set in the process. Unfortunately our caution was short-lived, and as I (?) yanked the comforter off the stand to put it back on the bed, well, you know what happened. **CRASH!** The work of art lay broken and destroyed on the floor.

I don't know what happened next, but I have a half-inch-long scar on the inside of my forearm to remind me that I shed some blood, and probably some fear-tears in the ensuing moments, as we picked up the pieces, and had to face my mother with the evidence. I don't remember being reprimanded or punished, but I certainly felt remorse, even though at the time I didn't have that word in my vocabulary.

There are a lot of 'Ooops!' events in our lives. We don't mean for them to happen, but in moments of distraction or haste, even a brief lapse in concentration, things happen. In a loving setting, it's not a big deal, and is quickly forgiven and forgotten. (We can even forgive ourselves, and laugh it off). In some environments it sets off accusation, name-calling, anger, rage, harsh punishment, and an ongoing blame-game. The result is wounded emotions, deep hurts that don't heal, resentment, self-condemnation, dysfunction and depression, often with a continuation of the wrong behavior into the next generation. If I am describing your life, let me encourage you to go to God with your hurts. Give them to Him, and forgive and pray blessings on the ones who hurt you (Matt.5:44). If possible find a church or ministry where deliverance is practiced, so that the generational iniquities can be stopped with *you*, enabling both you and your children, and your children's children to live in God's peace, love and blessing. This is your heritage in Christ, as God's children! (Eph.1:11-14).

12
PIGSTY TO PLAYHOUSE

It was a very exciting adventure for this little seven-year old "country mouse" to leave the farm, and move to town with her family. Overnight we had a new house, new school, new friends, and a whole new way of life, in this amazing community of maybe 200 inhabitants. Dad had purchased twenty-two acres of land on the edge of town, to accommodate the "farm" we brought with us – a few cows to supply milk, chickens for their eggs, and horses as a means of transport and source of income. Stands of poplar trees surrounding small ponds provided shelter and water for the animals, as well as a natural playground for the children. There was plenty of room for pasture for the livestock, and also for the large garden of vegetables, and field of sweet corn that were lovingly planted and tended each summer, to feed the family, and share with others.

I can't remember having pigs in town, but a converted pigsty became a treasure that gave many hours of pleasure to me and my siblings. Play-house size, it sat in our yard, its gray, weather-worn boards revealing its former 'life'. But, in our imaginations it became whatever we wanted it to be on any particular day or at any time. I doubt we ever thought of it as a pigpen, because we transformed it into a hospital, complete with doctor, nurse and patient; or a school where we taught/ learned the skills of reading, writing and arithmetic; a church filled with singing and preaching; a Sunday School where we stressed memorization of Bible verses; a store, using left-over ration coupons from WWII as money; or a house, with a Daddy, a Momma and 'model' children. We might have a wedding one day, or a funeral the next. We didn't have a lot of props, or much reality, but we were happy, and thankful for this special place where we could play and explore, enjoying the gifts each one brought into the scene.

On a much grander scale, God takes <u>us</u> as we are and trans-forms us into something that gives Him immense pleasure (1 Cor.6:11; Eph.1:4-6). WOW!! When we accept Jesus as our Savior and Lord, He puts the treasure of His very life into the clay vessels that are our bodies, so that we become the temple of the Holy Spirit (2 Cor.4:6-7; 1 Cor.6:19-20). Isn't this amazing?

The possibility of what God can do in us and with us is as unlimited as God's imagination. {Remember, He created the heavens, the earth and everything in and beyond these! (Gen.1)} What we become is only limited by our measure of yieldedness to Him, in obedience and purity (Jer.29:11-13; Luke 1:37-38; Rom.6:13-19). God does not transform us by dressing up the outside; it's an inside job, in our mind and in our spirit. (Rom.12:1-2; 2 Cor.3:17-18). Does He have your permission to renovate and restore you?

13
'DADDY!'

n the months before our move off the farm, my father had spent many days away from home, building a new house for his family in town. Our moving day was December 2, 1944, and the cold Saskatchewan winter had already set in. I was excited, and awed at what Daddy had made – a two-storied frame house for *us,* as well as a barn for the animals. As I child I wasn't concerned that the house was unfinished. It had no foundation, no indoor plumbing or running water. Central heating consisted of a large wood/coal stove in approximately the center of the ground floor. The upstairs was just bare rafters–sans ceiling, sans insulation, sans inside walls or doors (never did get the walls and doors!). We accessed it by ladder – the stair steps came later. The hot stove pipe ran through this open area, until the brick chimney was later built (after the next summer, when the basement was dug and the house moved onto a concrete foundation).

All this to set the scene for a special memory. Sometimes as a child I would wake up in the night due to a tummy-ache, a fear, or a bad dream. Without hesitation I would call out: "Daddy!", in a whisper at first; and if there was no answer, I would call again, louder, more insistent, my voice echoing through the open space, until I heard a stirring downstairs. As soon as I knew he had heard me, I would feel safe and comforted.

Waiting until I saw his head appear above the stair opening, I would then 'fly' to the shelter of his strong arms. Without a word, he would carry me downstairs, and I was soon relishing the comfort and safety of his nearness, his arm around me with a perfect father-love that banished all my fears. I could feel his heartbeat, and hear him breathing, each exhaled breath making a little whistling sound, and caressing my head with warmth. With a contented sigh I would fall asleep—all was well!

As I wrote the last paragraph, my eyes were blurred with tears, and I was sobbing at the precious reminder of how much love my father had for me, and for each one of his fourteen children. If a human father can love like this, how much more deeply does our perfect Father God love His children! He tells us "I have loved you with an everlasting love; therefore with loving-kindness I have drawn you" (Jer.31:3). "Behold what manner of love the Father has bestowed on us, that we should be called children of God" (1 John 3:1). "God so loved . . . that He gave His only begotten Son", to "redeem us from every lawless deed and purify for Himself His own special people" (John 3:16; Tit.2:14). God wants you to **know** His love, not just know *about* it! (Rom.5:5; Eph.3:16-19, 1 John 4:18) Call out His name, ABBA (Daddy) today, and flee to His waiting arms!

14
RUNAWAY!

$\mathcal{T}$he basement had been dug, the concrete outer walls and water cistern were completed, and it was time to move the house onto this foundation. My Dad had cleverly rigged a set of pulleys and ropes, that made it possible for a single team of horses, under his direction, to move the house, position it, and pull it up a ramp, and onto the concrete. Family and neighbors gathered around to watch the amazing feat. Cheers for a job well done!

The horses had worked hard, and were resting at the edge of the crowd, when suddenly something spooked them, and they bolted, still hitched together, joined by the singletree, with reins dangling. Somebody shouted "**Runaway!**", and the horses galloped through the crowd. My older sister was standing near my little brother who was lying in his baby carriage, and she could see that he was in the horses' path. Her quick reaction to the danger probably saved his life, as she stood her ground to veer them off. She was definitely the hero of the day!

The horses, still racing wildly, left the yard, tore down the lane, and crossed the road into a large, marshy vacant lot. For whatever purpose, there was a tall metal pipe standing in their path, and they apparently each chose to run on a different side of the pipe, thus slamming into it with the singletree, effectively bringing them to an abrupt and probably painful halt!

Let's learn a lesson from the runaway team. Fear of something, real or imagined, can set us on a destructive course, which can cripple us, and hurt those who cross our paths. Fear is often irrational, and affects our ability to think or act sanely. We do things we would never do under normal circumstances. We make choices, often knee-jerk reactions, just like the horses did, that will either destroy us, or bring us up short. I have no idea what went through the minds of those horses at their moment of reality. I do know that we as a family were grateful that they survived, unhurt, for future service, and that they caused no physical harm to anyone while in their crazed state of panic.

God intervened on behalf of our family on that memorable day, to protect us, and others. He is our only reliable deliverance from fear, as David knew so well. Hear these words from the Psalms he wrote: ""Whenever I am afraid I will trust in You . . . In God I have put my trust; I will not fear" (Psa.56:3-4); "The angel of the LORD encamps around all those who fear Him, and delivers them (Psa.34:7). If you are filled with fear, read Psa.91. Meditate on the truths and claim the promises over and over, until in that secret place of His loving presence, you can rest, unafraid. His perfect love casts out fear! (1 John 4:18) Live in His peace!

15
SUFFERING IN SILENCE

*W*hen I was growing up in small-town Saskatchewan, the local highway ran through the middle of town. It wasn't paved—just a narrow graveled road, with not a lot of traffic. One of the rules of our house was that no one was to ride a bicycle on the highway. For our protection, it was off limits. But I had quite a streak of rebellion in me, and one day in defiance of the 'law,' took the bike onto the forbidden road. I hadn't pedaled very far, when, while rounding a corner, suddenly the loose stones caught the tires in a vicious skid. The bike and I crashed and slid into the stones, landing in a most undignified heap.

I struggled to my feet, picked up the bike, and assessed the situation. The bike seemed fine, but I was hurting. The worst part was, I knew I had disobeyed, and no one, especially my parents, could know. Like Adam after eating the forbidden fruit, I was afraid, guilty and ashamed. I pushed the bike home, and went to my room to examine my stinging wounds. The outer part of my right leg, from knee to waist, was devoid of skin—raw exposed flesh—not a pretty sight! I knew I had to protect my secret, to avoid scolding or punishment; but also there would be no sympathy or healing treatment. So I suffered in silence!

I would like to say that was the last of my rebellion, but it wasn't. Had I gone to my parents and admitted my disobedience, things might have been much different. I could have experienced their loving care and concern, and best of all, their forgiveness. In the future, this might have kept me from hurting them further by my selfish actions. It took another sixty years before I understood the freedom and release of repentance and forgiveness of sin. As I allowed God's Spirit to search out the hidden iniquity and sin of my heart, His goodness led me to repentance (Psa.139:23-24; Heb.4:13; Rom.2:4). The reason I was able to do this was because I finally knew, in my heart of hearts, that God loves me beyond comprehension, and without condemning, wants me to be rid of the garbage from my past that keeps me bound by fear, shame and guilt (1 John 1:8–2:2). I finally could live the abundant life Jesus came to give all who trust in Him (John 10:10).

Do you sometimes find yourself thinking evil thoughts? Do you ever suddenly lash out at people with anger, criticism, judgment and accusation? Are you plagued by depression or bitterness? Ask God to show you where the evil spirits behind these things were given a door into your soul, through your sin or the sins of others. As He shows you the sin, take responsibility for it, and turn from it in repentance. Then cast out those spirits in the name of Jesus. Take back the peace, joy, and well-being the enemy has stolen from you, and enter into God's freedom (John 10:10; Heb.2:14-15; John 8:32, 36; Gal.5:1).

16
THAT MISSING PIECE

A highlight for me as a child was a special Christmas and New Year's tradition. Not everyone shared my enthusiasm, but I could hardly wait for someone to produce that shiny new box with a picture on top, and open it up to spill out hundreds of jig-sawed pieces which would keep us occupied for several hours, recreating the image on the box. It was more than just a puzzle to be solved. It was an exciting challenge, fitting all those pieces together to make something beautiful, to bring order out of chaos, and wholeness out of fragmentation.

What really *puzzled* me was the different methods of attack used by different people. We mostly agreed that the pieces should all be turned right-side-up first, and edge pieces extracted for the next step – making a border for the rest of the picture. But then, some would randomly pick up a piece, and search for a place for it, trying it here, there or wherever, in hopes it would eventually fit somewhere. This created a maze of hands, arms and shadows that resembled a game of twister. In defense, I learned to choose a few pieces of similar color, and find a spot outside the border to create a part of the picture, and at the right time to transplant it where it belonged. I also found that looking for a missing piece allowed me to use my eyes to discern by the shape and color whether it would fit in the empty spot, rather than having to manually experiment with numerous pieces.

Did you ever come to the end of the pieces before the puzzle was finished? Of course there might be one or two participants who have hidden a piece, so they can have the pleasure of completing the picture. But, if not, and there is a hole with no piece to fill it, it is very disappointing! It's like a hole in your heart, with no *peace* to fill it. The rest of your life might look great, but all you can focus on is that gaping vacancy. You try to fill it with things that don't fit, or close your heart so you and others can't see its lack, or so that no more pieces will be stolen.

As God fits together the pieces of our life, sometimes in our busy-ness we may lose sight of things we need to complete the picture – like that close fellowship with God, in prayer and the Word (1 John 1:6-7). Or we listen to the voice of the enemy who comes to kill our hope, steal our joy and destroy our peace (John 10:10). God is the only one who can make our lives complete (Col.2:10; 2 Tim.3:16-17). Notice in Heb.13:20-21 that it is the God of peace who completes you. God Himself is the missing 'peace' (1 Thes.5:23). If you have crowded Him out, invite Him, with a sincere heart of repentance, to come and heal your heart with His love and peace, joy and hope (Rom.5:1-2, 5).

17
KNOTS

$\mathcal{O}$ne thing I enjoyed as a child was embroidering. My mother had some beautiful pieces of embroidery she had done, and they inspired me to learn from her. I loved the feel of the silky threads and it was fun choosing the right colors from a wide assortment of bright hues. The way the embroidery hoops stretched the cloth as tight as a drum totally fascinated me. And there was such a sense of accomplishment as the design began to appear in response to my busy needle going through the cloth over and over again, following the stenciled pattern.

One of the first things I had to learn was how to make a knot that would not slip through the cloth. It had to be on the underside, out of sight, but would act as an anchor for the thread as it was tugged in and out through the cloth to create the picture. Knots are not to be seen, I thought. Then along came the lesson on the French knot. Apparently it has enough style to make the front page! French knots add a raised texture to the design, and are used, for example, to depict the little anthers in flowers. It took a while to learn the technique of twisting the thread around the needle two or three times, close to the point, and then poking the needle through to the back, leaving the twisted thread on the top like a tiny frosting-flower on a cake. Neat!

What about the knots in our *life*? We all have them, don't we? We know there are good knots, if we want to fasten something securely–ask a sailor or a cowboy! But do you like a knot in your shoelace, or your muscle? Nasty life-knots can happen when our plans go awry, and it feels like our neck is in a noose; when we get a bad diagnosis from the doctor and we feel a tightening around our heart; when we are criticized or accused, and huge knots appear in our gut. The common thread here is anxiety and fear. Fear of the future, fear of illness or death and fear of people are just a few examples of fears that bind us and cripple us. How can we undo these knots of fear and anxiety?

Ask these questions, and answer them thoughtfully and honestly.

–Am I trusting God for my future, or making my own plans?
–Do I believe what God says, or man's opinion?
–Is this fear and anxiety from God or from the enemy?
–Can I release my accusers to God, and forgive them?
–Have I learned to bless those who hurt me, not curse them?
–Does God really love me, and am I accepting His love?
–Will I give myself in complete surrender to God and His will?
–Am I ready to repent of my fears, and receive forgiveness?
–Are there things in my past that are holding me captive?
–Do I understand that God wants me to be free and healed?
–Do I <u>want</u> to be free and healed of past hurts?

Read Psa.103:2-5; Isa.61:1-3; 2 Tim.1:7; Phil.4:6-7; Eph.3:14-21.

18
I CAN SEE! I CAN SEE!

I don't know when it first manifested, but with each successive year in my early school days, I had to sit closer to the front of the room in order to read from the blackboard. Near-sightedness, or myopia, was a fact of life that I accepted, not considering it much of an issue. I just compensated, and carried on. When I was twelve, a health nurse visited our school, and tested my eyes. Apparently there was a deal where I could get free glasses, which would be sent to me through the mail. As the time passed, I remember going to the Post Office after school every day, until finally the package arrived. I dashed out of the building, while tearing at the wrapping, and opened the box to behold a pair of round, metal-rimmed glasses—not the most attractive, but what did I expect for nothing?

My eagerness to see what would happen when I put them on overcame my disappointment in the style, and there, on small-town Main Street, I suddenly had a whole new view of life. A girl was walking half a block or so ahead of us, and I shouted ecstatically, "That's Lizzie—I can see her! I can see who she is!" What had been a faceless form suddenly had an identity. This was truly amazing! All the way home, I kept exclaiming at everything I could recognize that for years was just a blob on the horizon. How much I had missed!

Fast-forward sixty years. Another free gift came to me, when a friend approached me at church. God had directed her to give me a book she had paid a dollar for at a liquidation store a few months earlier. As I opened that book* and began to read, I wasn't impressed with the author's style, but suddenly it was as if cataracts were removed from my spiritual eyes. **I could see in a whole new dimension –** who I am (*my identity in Christ*), who God is (*my loving Father*), who others are (and *that I can see past their sin and love them*), and how our inter-relationships had been fractured by sin. I also recognized our mutual enemy, Satan, as *real*, and *determined to steal, kill and destroy us with lies, accusations and curses on our lives (John 10:10).*

Along with this came the **insight** that spiritual issues are the root of most diseases, and God's design is that we be well (Psa.103:3). *When we recognize, repent of, and renounce our sins (including generational iniquities); forgive all who wronged us; receive God's forgiveness; and in Jesus' Name cast out the evil spirits behind the sins; our fellowship with God, ourselves and others is restored. As a result, our body comes into peace, and begins to function in the way it was made to do, bringing health and restoration (1 John 1:6-9; 4:4; Matt.10:1; 3 John 2). AMEN!*

*" A More Excellent Way Be in Health" by Henry W. Wright

19
A NEW FLAVOR

There was an unspoken rule in our house, that when Mom was cooking, everyone stayed out of the kitchen. Our responsibilities as older children began after the meal – clearing the table, doing the dishes, and cleaning up the kitchen. But on Saturday we could bake cakes or cookies, usually on our own. One incident of my cookie-making efforts will go down in the family history. Things were going great and I popped my first sheet of cookies in the oven. But, soon a strange smell began to permeate the air, and it seemed to be coming from the stove. The questions began. "Eunice, what are you making?" "Cookies". "What did you put in them?" "I just followed the recipe!" "Are you sure?"

I need to explain something here. Our neighbor was a travelling salesman of Watkins products, and Mom frequently bought some of their flavorings, etc. The bottles containing the products were uniform in size and shape—and here I will continue the cookie saga. The recipe called for a teaspoon of vanilla extract, so I reached up into our all-purpose cupboard, grabbed a bottle, and measured a teaspoonful of liniment into the mixing bowl. That's correct – liniment – a highly aromatic medicinal liquid that is rubbed into the skin to relieve muscle pain or stiffness. I put *that* into my cookies! The house smelled like a Sloan's factory. It was an excusable error – the bottles looked alike; but obviously I hadn't read the label, or detected the unusual odor.

We didn't waste much at our house, and the bravest of us ate the cookies, in spite of the odd taste. We rationalized that the liniment couldn't harm us, might even be beneficial??

In the grand scheme of things, mistaking liniment for vanilla is fairly benign. On a more serious note, our adversary, the devil, is a master of deception, even imitating works of God, to deceive God's people (Matt.24:24). He often comes as an angel of light, to make evil look good, and good evil (2 Cor.11:14; Isa.5:20). He distorts the truth of God to bring doubt into our minds, and pull believers away from the true gospel (Gen.3:4-5; Gal.1:6, 3:1; Col.2:8, 18). We need to know the truth of God's Word, so we recognize the counterfeit, and not be deceived by any imitation of the truth (2 Tim.3:13-17; 2:23-26; Josh.1:8).

In his second letter, Peter confirms the truth of Paul's teaching, and warns that untaught and unstable teachers twist the hard-to-understand teachings of Paul, and of all scripture, to their own destruction, and <u>we must be on guard</u> (2 Pet.3:15-18). As you open God's word, ask the Holy Spirit to guide you into all truth. This is one reason He was given to live within us, God's people (John 16:13). Do not be deceived by lies masquerading as truth!

20
THORNS

*O*ne of my most fondly remembered summer activities while growing up was picking juicy saskatoons and wild raspberries in the nearby river valleys. One day, however, I encountered a thorn bush (I think it was similar to the one the Roman soldiers used to plait the infamous 'crown of thorns' for the head of Jesus before His crucifixion). The thorns on 'my' bush were about two inches long, so when one of those spikes drove itself into my shin like a hypodermic needle, I felt it! But I backed off and bravely continued filling my pail with berries, soon forgetting all about it.

A few weeks later, I noticed a small sore on my leg. It was almost like a boil, but different. Obviously something was festering under the skin, with increasing redness, soreness and oozing pus. One day, as I was trying to coax some of this putrefaction out by pressing hard on the area surrounding the site, suddenly something shot out of the wound "something brown, about ¾" long, and sharp on one end. It was one of those "Aha" moments, as I realized that the long forgotten thorn that had pierced me, must have broken off in my leg, and had probably been firmly embedded in my shinbone, to eventually fester and beal, causing distress until pressured to leave. But now it was gone, and the wound immediately began to heal, leaving no scar.

The thorns and barbs of unkind words, emotional abuse, accusation and bullying often enter deep into our spirit as a child, (or adult), and may lie there for years, embedded in our psyche, and often forgotten. But sooner or later, they fester, and begin to resurface. They may manifest in negative emotions, such as anger, hatred or jealousy. We may have deep feelings of bitterness or rejection. There may be irrational fears. Sometimes our mental well-being is affected by these things, resulting in schizophrenic behavior or depression. Physical symptoms such as digestive problems and arthritis may appear.

We try to treat these symptoms with drugs or therapy, to no avail. But, as we learn to turn to the Lord about our illnesses and moods; and as we ask the Holy Spirit to show us if there is any spiritual root causing the disease or condition, He will show us. He will bring to our remembrance times where traumas have opened the door to spirits of rejection, fear, pain, etc. that have fractured who we are, causing our bodies to function improperly, resulting in disease. As we repent of sins such as bitterness and fear, casting out these evil spirits in the name of Jesus, and as we ask God to heal the wounds of the traumas, we will find the peace of heart and soul that will result in mental and physical healing and wholeness. Truly, we don't have to live with these nasty "thorns in the flesh". God wants us well! (3 John 2, Psa. 103:2-5; 1 Pet.2:24). Are we going to believe God for deliverance or continue to live in the bondage of the enemy? Choose life!

21
PIE CRUST

*W*hen I was in my 'teens', a group from our church was driving to a Bible Camp about ninety kilometers away, to drop off campers and food donations. I had been asked to bake two pies, which I was quite willing to do. If I remember, they were saskatoon-rhubarb, which is a wonderful-tasting combination! Let me insert right here that I don't much like the crust that comes with pies (unless it's made from cookie crumbs!) I wonder which came first – my dislike of *eating* the usual flour-and-shortening crust, or of actually *making* the crust. Maybe both negative things were determining factors in how the crusts turned out. Perhaps I tried too hard to get those circles just right, and the excess handling of the dough wasn't a good idea. My family was pretty forgiving if the crust was a bit tough, although I got ribbed about it.

But this time was different – people I didn't even know would be eating these pies – they had to be perfect. After careful effort the pies were assembled. They were beautiful, with fluted edges and a neat pattern of breathing-slits on top. But even as I waited for them to bake, I just knew the crust would be tough, even tougher than usual. Fears haunted me, until the next day. Then they became real, as I watched people struggling to cut through that crust, and giving up. (At least the filling was good!)

Since that time, I have never found a good reason to learn how to make a tender, flaky crust, although I admire and applaud those who can. However, I have learned a few things about fear—how it can grip you, tie you in knots, make you physically sick and paralyze you. If you focus on a fear of something happening long enough, it will probably happen (it becomes self-fulfilling). Do you remember what Job said after calamity struck his life and family? "The thing I greatly feared has come upon me, and what I dreaded has happened to me" (Job 3:25). Don't think that Satan wasn't involved. He had seen those burnt offerings Job made day after day, in *fear* that his grown children might have sinned (Job 1:5). So he orchestrated a plot to make those fears a reality (Job 1:1-2:7). (Most things we worry about never happen, thankfully!)

And what about perfectionism? Most would say it's a good thing. But could it be built on fear of not being loved, of not measuring up, of failure and embarrassment, perhaps even fear of people? Perfectionists become performance driven, over-achievers, *and* candidates for long-term debilitating illnesses such as chronic fatigue syndrome and fibromyalgia, where the overstressed body is forced out of the 'rat race' because of unexplained pain. If this describes you, take heed to the words of Jesus in Matt.11:28-29. Give Him your fears and burdens and receive His rest!

22
NONCONFORMIST

Dad told me once that I was a nonconformist, and I'm sure he meant it in the nicest sense of the word. I think I was old enough at the time to know what the word meant, and that it could have various connotations. (He could have called me a maverick, eccentric, or disobedient!) Somehow I was okay with the word he chose. I don't recall the incident that prompted his comment, but it was likely tied to what he added, that if there was a different way to do something, I would find it. Or maybe it was a polite way of saying I was stubborn, and a rebel at heart. Why did I zig when everyone else was zagging?

Whatever his meaning, I have since appreciated that he noticed something different about me, and loved me enough to tell me. I decided it was okay if I wore clothing that wasn't in style, and not let it matter what anyone thought or said. I wasn't obligated to drink coke or coffee just because everyone else did. I don't need my house to be glutted with dust-gathering gadgets, gizmos and gourmet cookbooks. I have decided I am unique. Isn't everyone? So, maybe I'm more unique than others. I'm fine with that, as I have learned to accept *me* the way I am, and to not try to fit in at any cost, especially if it would compromise my walk with God!

In Rom.12: 2, Paul pleads with us as Christ-followers not to be conformed to this world. In other words, we are not to let this world's focus, or system or way of life become ours. Where the world is concerned we are to be nonconformists! We have been *called out of this world*, to become citizens of heaven (John 15:19; Phil.3:20; Jas.4:4). Our new citizenship should be evident by the way we live, under new leadership (2 Cor.6:14-18). The second part of Rom.12:2 shows us how this is possible: "Be <u>transformed</u> by the renewing of your mind." We need a new mindset, a complete makeover in our thinking, a mind focused on God, and <u>His</u> kingdom (Matt.6:33, Col.3:1-2). We must let the Holy Spirit and the Word of God transform our mind with truth, in order to think, speak and act like a child of our Father God!

I said earlier that I accept myself for who I am, i.e. the way God made me (Psa.139:14). But, I know I have been flawed by sin. As my Creator, God has the right to continue to correct, change and improve me, to <u>conform</u> me more and more <u>to His likeness</u>! (Rom.8:29; 2 Cor.3:18). He will, as I yield myself to Him as a living sacrifice (Rom.12:1). "We have the mind of Christ"! (I Cor.2:16)

> "He who has begun a good work in you will complete it until the day of Jesus Christ." Phil.1:6

> "For it is God who works in you both to will and to do of His good pleasure." Phil.2:13

23
CONNECTIONS

I was probably around fifteen when my parents took on the job of operating the local telephone switchboard, which meant moving part of the family into the house where the telephone office was located. As well as Mom and Dad, three of us girls learned the lingo, and how to connect the local people, by telephone, with others in the community, or in another city or country. The operator's chair faced a panel of numbered holes, one for each local line, plus separate ones for long distance calling. There was a series of single-pronged plugs lined up in pairs like soldiers across the desk. When a call would come in, we had to grab one of the plugs from a pair, and place it in the hole in the panel, where the light was blinking (signifying which line the caller was on). Pushing a switch allowed us to hear and talk to the person calling. (Is this pretty simple compared to today's technology, or does it sound more complicated?)

After determining whom they wanted to speak with, we would take the matching plug from the pair, plug it in to the correct line, and do a sort of coded ring by pulling on the ringer trigger. When the person came on line, we would flip the switch for the final connection. Now communication could flow!

Before the death of Jesus on the cross, the connection between God and His people seemed very complicated.

There were the laws of cleansing, the numerous sacrifices, tithes and offerings. And only the High Priest could go into the Holy of Holies, beyond the veil of the temple, where God was, and that only once a year. Yet, there were some like Moses, David and Daniel who realized God would hear their cries for help from a repentant heart.

When Jesus called out from the cross, "It is finished", "the veil of the temple was torn in two from top to bottom" (Matt.27:51). His own flesh was the torn veil that opened access for us to Father God. Ponder these precious words from Heb.10:19-22: "Therefore, brethren, having boldness to enter the Holiest by the blood of Jesus, by a new and living way which He consecrated for us through the veil, that is, His flesh, and having a High Priest over the house of God, let us draw near with a true heart in full assurance of faith." Heb.4:16 says "Let us come boldly to the throne of grace, that we may obtain mercy and find grace to help in time of need." And in Rom.5:1-2 we read: "Therefore, having been justified by faith, we have peace with God through our Lord Jesus Christ, through whom we have access by faith into this grace in which we stand." Now THAT is a great connection! Are *you* on the open line to God? Unlimited calling by innumerable people—no busy signal! And the cost has been prepaid by Jesus!

24
LEAVING THE NEST

The last year of High School was drawing to a close, and as I prepared for Graduation ceremonies and studied for final exams, my teacher was making plans for me to obtain a scholarship to attend university. But, at barely seventeen I wasn't ready for that big leap. My sister was making application to attend a small Bible School, and this seemed like a better choice for me as well. This did not please my teacher, who said I was throwing away my life, or at least a great opportunity. But, if I had to leave the security of home, having my sensible, stable sister with me would make it less traumatic. We were both like naïve "babes in the woods", but we could make it together.

And so began a whole new adventure. I diligently applied myself to my studies, but I couldn't help noticing all the cute guys. Being from a small town, where there weren't any nice Christian boys to get to know, I had never dated. Bible School rules did not permit dating, but this did not keep me from dreaming, and hoping that I just might catch someone's attention. I actually did, and even though he wasn't the one I had my eye on, I let myself be drawn in by his interest. But two months out of school, I called it off, unwilling to stop school for a man I didn't really love.

After two more years, and another graduation, it was time once again to make further career plans. My sister was looking to go as a missionary to Colombia, while I hoped to get training to be a school teacher. So, we parted ways, but I have always been glad for her patience with my shenanigans as we both received a good foundation in Bible knowledge there, and learned to live and serve in a Christian community.

One of the main reasons I was thankful for the decision to attend Bible School after High School was that it helped to solidify and stabilize my faith, and generally prepare me for life. I regret that in my case at least, a lot of it was just head knowledge, that didn't reach my heart and become worked out in my life. I feel a loss in not being taught more about spiritual warfare, and about living a victorious life through the baptism of the Holy Spirit and in His power, instead of struggling in my own strength to keep a set of rules, and failing so often. I wish I had known that God still heals, and works other miracles today, and He desires us to live in wholeness, wellness and abundant life.

> "The thief (Satan) does not come except to steal, and to kill, and to destroy. I (Jesus) have come that they may have life, and that they may have it more abundantly." (John 10:10)

> "The kingdom of God is . . . righteousness and peace and joy in the Holy Spirit." (Rom.14:17)

25
~~T.B.~~

$\mathcal{O}$n the late 1950's, in order to earn money to attend Teachers' college, I worked for a year in a tuberculosis sanitarium in Fort San, in Saskatchewan's Qu'Appelle Valley. Now, in 2013, T.B. is supposedly eradicated in North America. Not so then, nor in many countries around the world today. Several hundred T.B. patients were hospitalized in the Fort San center—men, women and children. Most were there for months, longing for the day when they would be cured and able to go back home.

For those who may not know, T.B. is caused by a bacterium, for which effective antibiotics have now been developed. T.B. used to be called 'the wasting disease', and 'consumption', which indicates how serious a threat it was. Symptoms displayed as loss of weight, energy and appetite, a persistent cough, and night sweats. It was very infectious, spread typically by coughing. The disease commonly invaded the lungs, which would fill with mucous and gradually waste away, limiting breathing. However, it could also attack other parts of the body, such as the stomach, bones, or lymphatic system, causing pain and death. It is one of the most insidiously destructive diseases known to man.

T.B. bacteria may live in a person's body for years, then manifest its symptoms when the immune system has been compromised, and can no longer fight back. That is why it often claims people who are vulnerable – the homeless, poor, and underprivileged. In a similar way, a spirit of death, or of infirmity, of fear, or bitterness can hide undetected in a person's soul for years; but in a moment of weakness and vulnerability, it breaks loose and begins to torment, causing dis-ease and dysfunction in the body and mind, plus spewing out to infect those around us with our hurtful anger and words. Often, we do not know how to fight back, or how to be healed and delivered (Rom.7:14-24).

Every day, at Fort San, the orderlies would roll the patients in their beds, out onto the open balconies, to breathe the cold, fresh, unpolluted air into their diseased lungs for a few hours. So while the antibiotics fought the bacteria, the oxygen worked at restoring health to the damaged lungs. As in the physical, so it is in the spiritual. Along with resisting and casting out the evil spirits that manifest, by the powerful name of Jesus, we need the Holy Spirit, God's breath of life, to renew our minds through the Word. In this way, our Spiritual immune system is built up, the lies of Satan are replaced by the truth of God, and the tissues of our life are restored, to function as God intended for them to do. See Jas.4:7-8; Eph.6:11; Rom.12:2, Tit.3:5; Psa.1:2-3, 107:20.

26
ARTISTS

*T*hroughout the years of my education, I encountered several opportunities to explore the world of an artist. It likely began with wax crayons or plasticine (modeling clay), then branched out to include pencil sketching, painting with water colors, and making paper snowflakes. At Teachers College I tried my hand at leather tooling and pottery. It didn't take long for me (and my teachers) to realize that an artist I was not, and never hoped to be. However I do appreciate and marvel at those who are able to create beauty out of ordinary things, and draw things that actually look real. (I'm not so much into the abstract concept). At the same time, I cannot ignore the lessons to be learned from artists. Art is creativity, and reflects the likeness of the Creator in His creatures who are made in His image.

Painters who work with oils start by procuring a canvas of the desired size and texture, made usually from cotton or linen. To make a canvas more endurable and permanent, for a longer-lasting painting, it is stretched over a wooden frame and stapled on to the frame to keep it taut. Probably most painters have a picture planned in their mind, and possibly as they look at the blank canvas, they don't see the dull, coarse, nondescript rectangle of canvas, but the beautiful masterpiece it will become beneath their brush. If we were to watch an artist at work, we may disagree with his choice of color, or wonder why he daubs instead of brushing, or can't imagine how it will look when he's finished. We just need to remember that it's *his* work, and he knows what he's doing. Before long the canvas is transformed into a thing of beauty, to be framed in gold or bronze, perhaps, and put on display for the world to see. The artist takes pride in his work, and receives the praise worthy of it.

God is the Master Artist, and we are His works of art. "We are His workmanship, created in Christ Jesus for good works, which God prepared beforehand that we should walk in them (Eph.2:10). The word workmanship suggests a poem or a design produced by an artisan. Just as the canvas cannot boast in, or take credit for the masterpiece the artist created, no more can we boast in what God has done in our lives. Nor can we argue with the Artist about what He's painting on the canvas of our life, or complain that we are stretched way out of our comfort zone. It is actually quite clear in Scripture that we were chosen, redeemed and sanctified for the glory and praise of God (Eph.1:3-6, 12-14; Phil.1:11). He has made beauty out of our blahs; he has taken the mundane and made it glorious. As we let Him choose the colors and the brush-strokes, the painting of our life will bring glory, and honor and praise to God, now and throughout eternity! AMEN!

27
LEAVES

As a new teacher, I taught in the bush country north of Prince Albert, at a school by the side of a highway. Most of the children hadn't seen many motor vehicles, so every time one went by, curious eyes peered out the windows. One September day, in Art class, we all went outdoors and collected leaves in various shapes and colors. These were then arranged on sheets of waxed paper, then another sheet was laid on top, and ironed onto the bottom sheet. One per window solved the distraction problem!

Speaking of hiding things with leaves, I really have a lot of questions about the Garden of Eden – like, how long did Adam and Eve live there before they were evicted? Did they sleep at night? Was the climate so perfect they didn't need any blankets? If not, why didn't they grab a blanket when they realized they were naked? Was there even such a thing as cloth, or any sort of fabric? Why did they choose fig leaves to cover their nakedness? What did they use to hold them together, or keep them on? What did these new fashion items look like? They've been called tunics, aprons, coverings . . . But I suppose if we really needed to know, we would have been told. I'm also thinking this could have been man's first invention, but it wasn't that great!

Actually, up until Eve was paid a visit by the evil liar, AKA Satan, or the devil, disguised as a serpent, there was no need for clothing. With the eating of the forbidden fruit, and the introduction of 'the knowledge of good and evil', suddenly nakedness was an issue that brought shame to the Eden couple. Ergo, they were in a panic to find something, *anything,* to cover up before the LORD God came to call on them. It seems that the fig leaf idea wasn't satisfactory, because they still hid themselves out of fear. Check out the story in Genesis 3.

Have you ever been so filled with shame, fear and guilt, that you couldn't face God, and so you ran away and hid from Him? Maybe you've been running and hiding for a long time, even for years. But, If you think about it, He already knows where you're hiding, why you're running, and the shame and guilt you feel. The truth is, He is not condemning you—<u>you</u> are condemning you! He is waiting for you to come out of the bushes and surrender to Him. As you do, He will eradicate your fear with His love, trade your shame for the righteousness of His Son, and replace your guilt with His glory. He is the safest One you could ever trust! His grace will displace your disgrace!

God gave Adam an opportunity to repent (Gen.3:11), but instead Adam shifted the blame, and so received the judgment. Admit your sin, shame, fear and guilt to God right now and receive His forgiveness, cleansing and renewal! (Acts 2:38; 1 John 1:9)

28
FIRE!

*T*he elementary school where I taught was housed in two one-room buildings next to the highway in northern Saskatchewan. We were in a grassy area, surrounded by the mostly-pine forest typical of the area. One afternoon we had settled back into the books, following break, when the relative quiet was shattered by the dreaded word "FIRE!" The roving eyes of one of the students had caught a glimpse of smoke through the window. We all sprang to our feet and ran outside, and to the back of the building. Someone ran to alert the teacher and students in the other building, and they spilled out to join us.

A sizable patch of the thick, long, dry grass was already engulfed in flame, and the wind was carrying it towards the timber. There were about fifty of us, including a few strong older boys, and we began pounding at the edges of the fire with our jackets—our only equipment. Some of the faster runners were dispatched to get help, while we continued to beat out the flames at the edge of the circle of fire, working our way inward, over the still-hot earth. We were relentless, spurred on by visions in our minds of a raging forest fire, unless we stopped the flames before they reached the trees. Help finally arrived, and we conquered!

A very penitent grade five student admitted to playing with firecrackers behind the school during break. Of course he didn't set out to cause a fire. He made an unwise decision, based on immaturity, the lure of excitement, and showing off to the other boys. He probably wasn't thinking of the consequences, beyond hoping he wouldn't get caught!

Can you relate to this story in some way? Have you made some decisions that you now regret? Are you still beating yourself up over it? Is it like an albatross around your neck, or like shackles on your ankles? Maybe you have repented many times, and still you feel shame or guilt. Please consider God's plea to His people in Isaiah 55:6-7. He says that as we seek the Lord, forsaking the ways and thoughts of an unrighteous person, and returning to the LORD, 'He will have mercy' on us and *'abundantly pardon'*.

This abundant pardon has been obtained for us through the cross of Christ (Heb.10:10). If we do not accept the forgiveness of God, we are saying Jesus' blood was not sufficient to cancel our debt of sin. If we do not forgive ourselves, when God has freely forgiven us, again we are trampling on His grace, saying it is not enough to erase our sin as well as our regrets. Repent of unforgiveness towards yourself, and of carrying the shame and guilt He died to free you from. Receive forgiveness! Bury the albatross and the shackles! Walk in freedom into your future, to be all God has planned for you to be (Jer.29:11-13; Gal.5:1).

29
FLYING

A few weeks after arriving in Montreal Lake, I made a trip out, for a week-end Conference at the Bible School I had attended. I arranged for a small plane to fly out from Prince Albert, and take me back there, to catch another plane to Regina. The little two-seater training-Cessna landed in a snow-covered clearing in the dense bush. With no room to maneuver for take-off, the pilot got out and manually turned the plane around! Soon we were air-borne on my first flying experience. A light snow was falling, so we flew low, barely above the tree-tops, frequently experiencing roller-coaster effect stomach-dropping air-pockets. It was fun!

I boarded a somewhat larger plane for the next leg of the trip, and flew much faster, higher and more smoothly. I was enjoying it until we began to descend. My ears hurt, and my head seemed about to burst with pain. I didn't know then that the denser air as we approach the earth causes pressure differences between the inside and outside of the eardrum. It's called barotrauma, and it certainly wasn't fun. I was slightly deaf for several days!

Different types of aircraft, from the huge Boeing Jumbo Jets to the sturdy DC-3 cargo planes, and even a helicopter have taken me many air-miles to exciting destinations over the years; and I must say it is my favorite way to travel. A few years ago, I flew from Calgary to visit missionary friends in

Thailand. As we rose and soared high above the earth, I glanced out the window and saw on the cloud below a silhouette of the plane inside a full-circle rainbow, moving along with the plane. Tears welled up in my eyes. It was as if God was assuring me with a rainbow token that He was in control of the plane, and I was safe.

It's always been an amazing physics mystery to me how such a heavy machine can defy gravity, rise to astounding heights, fly at crazy speeds for hours, then land on a precise piece of ground, under the control of one person. Like most people, I didn't wait until I understood how a plane works, before I boarded one, literally trusting the pilot and the plane with my life.

God's plan of Salvation, is by far the greatest, most profound and multifaceted mystery ever conceived. Our finite minds can never comprehend the **mystery** of the faith and godliness (1 Tim.3:9, 16); of God's will (Eph.1:9; Rom.11:25); of Christ (Col.4:3); of the Church (Eph.3:8-10; Col.1:26-27); of the Gospel (Eph.6:19); of the resurrection (1 Cor.15:51) or of iniquity (2 Thes.2:7). We do not need to understand how God works before we get on board with Him. As we believe God's Word, and trust Him for Salvation, He reveals these mysteries to us, and takes us on the best journey ever, to an indescribably beautiful destination. Are you ready?

30
FISHING

*D*uring the long cold winters in northern Saskatchewan, Montreal Lake is covered with several feet of ice. We would see tents of aboriginal people begin to appear along the shore, as the ice-fishing began. Sawing a hole down through the ice, they would ingeniously snake a large net along under the ice to a second hole, to catch the big White Fish, and perhaps some smaller Northern Pike and Pickerel found in abundance in the water below. These would quickly freeze in the sub-zero temperature, then be packed in ice for their journey south to be sold.

After the ice finally melts in the Spring, it is time for fly-fishing. Occasionally a few of us from the Mission Station would take a canoe or two out on the lake, casting lines to hopefully snag a tasty Pickerel, or at least a Pike. It was relaxing, and rewarding, as long as we weren't attacked too fiercely by mosquitoes, black flies and no-see-ums! We usually fished in the evenings, when the sun would shine as late as eleven o'clock. I can remember cleaning, cooking and consuming a Pickerel at a very late hour. It was so good, fresh from the lake. Once I felt like one of the rich and famous, as the fish I caught was full of eggs–caviar, which I cooked and ate (but didn't much like! I'm okay being ordinary!)

Fish were common in the fabric of the life of Jesus' followers, and featured in the teaching and miracles of the Master

Himself. Four fisherman were called to leave their nets and their livelihood to follow Jesus and become 'fishers of men' for the Kingdom. Two small fish along with five mini-loaves were multiplied to feed more than 5,000 people. After a wasted night with nary a nibble, Peter was overwhelmed with a net-stretching catch of 153 large fish, when he obeyed Jesus' command to cast on the other side of the boat. Peter was the one, also, who at Jesus' behest caught a fish, and found in its mouth enough money to pay both of their taxes! Jesus used the humble fish to display the miracle-working power of God. He proved His bodily resurrection from the dead by eating a piece of fish (Luke 24:39-43).

In the one parable featuring a fish, Jesus presumes that if a son asks his father for a fish, his father will not give him a serpent. He goes on to say "If you then, being evil, know how to give good gifts to your children, how much more will your heavenly Father give the Holy Spirit to those who ask Him!" (Luke 11:13) Indeed our loving Father knows how to give us, His children, perfect gifts (Jas.1:17). He wants to give us the precious gift of the baptism of His Holy Spirit. This gift was promised back in Joel 2:28-29; by John the Baptist (Luke 3:16) and by Jesus (Acts 1:4-5, 8). He came at Pentecost, to baptize with power and manifest signs and wonders. Let us not spurn this most treasured of all gifts!

31
THE CALL

*W*hen I was a child, missionaries to many lands often visited our little church. I was spellbound by their stories, and fascinated by the curios they displayed. One couple in particular impressed me, and the country they talked about really tugged at something in me. Even the name was musical – Ethiopia. Somehow I knew I would go there someday as a missionary, and this seemed to guide my steps through my late teens and early twenties, even though I didn't know how it would unfold. I guess I was waiting for a confirming 'call', but in the meantime, I prepared myself by attending Bible School as well as receiving teacher training. After Teachers College, I decided to go up north, to teach children at a Mission home that boarded children from remote areas while they attended the government school. I thought that would give me cross-cultural experience in an isolated situation, which it did.

During my third year at Montreal Lake, perhaps at Easter break, I attended a Revival Crusade in Saskatoon, featuring the Sutera Twins. I can remember weeping at the altar, as I rededicated my life to God, to serve Him wherever He led me. When I returned back north, I gave notice of resignation, and began to correspond with the Sudan Interior Mission, (now SIM International).

I was asked to attend Missionary Candidate School in Toronto in November of that year, where I was accepted to serve in Ethiopia as a career missionary-teacher. Then began months of travelling, making contacts with individuals and speaking in churches to raise support—something I didn't relish, but that had to be done before I could go out with the Mission. In between travel and speaking, I purchased supplies to last for five years—clothes, and basically everything needed to live. I packed in large steel barrels or drums that could be sealed and padlocked, as well as a small steamer trunk and a wooden crate. How I appreciated the help and support of my Dad in doing most of the hard work involved! When all was ready, we shipped them by transport truck to Toronto, where they were put on a ship for the sea journey of several weeks. In June I attended a Linguistics Course in Toronto, and in early September flew from there to Addis Ababa. What an adventure for this single 26-year old from the prairies! And it was only the beginning!

Before I left home, my church had a Commissioning service, sending me out with their support, prayers and blessing, even though it had been eight years since I had attended there, except occasionally. The Bible promise I chose and claimed was John 10:4 "And when He putteth forth His own sheep, He goeth before them" (KJV). It was reassuring to realize that the way was known to Him, and I did not need to fear what lay ahead!

32
LOSING CONTROL

*P*rior to leaving for Ethiopia I travelled by bus from North Battleford to Montreal Lake, to revisit the place and people where I had taught school for three years. One of the teachers was packing up to drive back to her home in North Battleford, and we arranged for me to go with her. At one point she asked me if I would drive for a while to give her a break. I agreed, because I did have my learner's license, and it was quite legal if she was in the passenger seat. As she sat munching on an apple, the gravel beneath my tires started to play havoc with my ability to steer the car where I wanted it to go. I felt an uneasy swaying (which she didn't seem to notice), and I knew I was losing control, fast. The fact is, I had already lost control. I remember briefly thinking this was 'the end'. Acting on this thought, I closed my eyes and jerked the steering wheel to the right, heading for the ditch, prepared to die. I felt the car flipping, once, twice? I don't know. Then it shuddered and was still. Was I in heaven?

My friend's panicked voice close to my ear was shouting, "Eunice, get off me. We have to get out. There's a fire under the hood!" My eyes flew open, and I was jerked back to reality. The car was in the ditch, passenger side down. It was a pre-seatbelt era, so I had slid down, pinning my friend beneath me. I realized that the half of the windshield in front of me had fallen out, leaving no shards of glass behind, just a beautiful escape hatch through which we quickly exited. A passing motorist got the hood open and threw dirt on the flame near the motor. After he went to get the police, we each picked a tire, and sat laughing hysterically, out of relief.

What can we do when things in life get out of control? Do we just give up? I think of David. From the time he was anointed to be the future king in Israel, until it actually happened, his whole life seemed to be out of control. He gathered a rag-tag group of men around him as a support group, but things went from bad to worse. Read 1 Sam.16 through to 2 Sam.4 to see what I mean.

It seems David was into journaling, writing down his thoughts, complaints, pleas for help, and praise to God in what we know today as the Psalms of David. He understood what <u>we</u> need to 'get', that ultimately God is the one and only answer to all of life's issues. Keeping our eyes on Him, and surrendering all our cares, burdens, needs and problems to Him, in thankful prayer, praise and worship, is exemplified by David in the Psalms, and commanded in Phil.4:6-7 with the attached promise of His peace. God wants you to give over the control of your life to Him, so *you* won't be concerned with having to keep things in control. Read a few Psalms each day, and ponder Jesus' words in Matt.6:25-34.

33
THE LAND OF EUCALYPTUS

*U*p until the time I went to Ethiopia in 1963, SIM missionaries travelled across the ocean by ship, a long and often tiresome trip. I was thankful that I was able to go by plane, especially since I would be travelling alone. I remember very little about that first journey to a new land and a new adventure. What I do recall, as I went by car from the airport, into the city of Addis Ababa in the early morning, was the aromatic smoke that filled the air. It rose lazily from hundreds of mud houses, where leaves and branches of eucalyptus trees crackled in small fires under clay coffee pots and cooking utensils. Inexplicably, it was sort of comforting, and made an indelible impression on my senses of sight and smell.

A bit of Wikipedia trivia tells me that eucalyptus trees, native to Australia, were introduced into Ethiopia in the early twentieth century by Jewish immigrants to plant in swamps, in order to stem the spread of insect-borne diseases. Another story claims they were brought in around 1895 to reforest the area around Addis Ababa, providing fuel and building materials. Perhaps both accounts are true. Over the years eucalyptus trees have become a very prominent part of the Ethiopian landscape and culture. The oil in their leaves also has many medicinal properties.

Trees form an integral part of Biblical truth. In the beginning they were created to produce seed-bearing fruit for our nourishment (Gen.1:29), and in the end, the leaves of the tree of life will heal the nations (Rev.22:2). Trees provide shelter, beauty and oxygen for our blessing and benefit, as well as fodder for many spiritual lessons. Here are a few of my favorites:

- "He (whose delight is in the law of the LORD) shall be like a tree planted by the rivers of water, that brings forth its fruit in its season, whose leaf also shall not wither; and whatever he does shall prosper." Psa.1:2-3
- "The righteous shall flourish like a palm tree; he shall grow like a cedar in Lebanon. Those who are planted in the house of the LORD shall flourish in the courts of our God. They shall still bear fruit in old age." Psa.92:12-14
- "The fruit of the righteous is a tree of life." Prov.11:30
- "A good tree cannot bear bad fruit, nor can a bad tree bear good fruit. By your fruits you will know them." Matt.7:18, 20 (What kind of fruit are we bearing?)
- "Himself (Jesus) bore our sins in His own body on the tree, that we, having died to sins might live for righteousness—by whose stripes you were healed." 1 Pet.2:24, Gal.3:13-14
- "To him who overcomes I will give to eat from the tree of life which is in the midst of the Paradise of God." Rev.2:7

34
CLIMBING

he town of Debre Birhan, where I spent nine months learning the beautiful but difficult Amharic language, lies next to the Rift Valley, which slices through Ethiopia's highlands like a jagged knife. The town is about 9,000 feet above sea level, so the air is thin and cold. Since we weren't doing strenuous physical work there, our lungs were able to handle its lower oxygen content. One Saturday, a group of us "foreigners" from several different countries went on a hike to explore this famous Rift Valley. As we looked into the valley, we could see a well-worn path snaking down the side of the escarpment, and we began our descent. We were still a long way from the floor of the valley, when we decided we should start back. As we did so we noticed below us in the far distance, a woman carrying a heavy load of dry tree branches on her back, coming up the narrow path towards us.

There's nothing like a steep climb at a high altitude to test the strength of a person's heart. We would advance a few steps, then stop to catch our breath and rest our aching legs. Our bodies screamed for oxygen, and our hearts worked desperately to catch enough of this precious element from our starving lungs to send out to the weakening muscles. It was a losing battle, and our only recourse was to listen to our bodies, resting long and frequently. We felt like wimps, even the strongest of us, as we panted and groaned our way slowly and painstakingly upward. To further emphasize our feebleness, the burden-bearing woman from below caught up to us, never missing a stride, without a hint of fatigue or shortness of breath. She greeted us and continued her climb, while we silently admired her stamina. We also silently decried our woefully short supply of endurance. What a strong, efficient heart this woman and her fellow country women and men develop as they live and work for years in the rarefied air of these highlands!

Isaiah's words come to mind: "He gives power to the weak, and to those who have no might He increases strength. Even the youths shall faint and be weary, and the young men shall utterly fall; but those who wait on the LORD shall renew their strength; they shall mount up with wings like eagles; they shall run and not be weary; they shall walk and not faint" (Isa.40:29-31).

It's easy to go downhill, even at a high elevation. It is the upward climb that requires strength and endurance. We don't have this in ourselves, and we can't muster it up. We have to depend on God and His strength in us. His Spirit will breathe into us the pure life-giving oxygen we need as we spend time with the LORD in prayer and the Word. "The people who know their God shall be strong and carry out great exploits" (Dan.11:32). AMEN!

35
HEE HAW, HEE HAW

*O*ne day soon after I arrived in Ethiopia, the silence around me was shattered by a loud, raucous, blood-curdling noise like none I had ever heard. The person with me laughed, and pointed out the window at the culprit—a small brown donkey, whose sides were heaving, as he drew breath in and out of his gaping mouth in repeated, drawn out EEEEEEE—AWWWWW's. How could so much noise come from such a gentle little creature, (compared to the soft whinny of his much larger, bolder cousin, the horse)? Apparently donkeys are social animals, and bray to communicate with humans, to attract attention, or in hopes of a response from another donkey. A bray can last twenty seconds, and be heard up to two miles away! That should frighten off any predators!

When I moved to my first Mission station, I sort of inherited a donkey, the beast of burden to haul water from the river, or food from the market. But he also was my lawn mower, and my yard was his home. In those days I owned a little cassette-recorder, so decided one day to get his braying on tape. As soon as I went outside he greeted me, and voila! His first recording! I pushed the 'Play' button to listen, and my 'lawn mower' responded to his own voice in kind, as often as I played the tape. What a racket!

We may not appreciate being likened to a donkey, but maybe we can learn from one. Donkeys are submissive to their master and obedient to his commands (Jas.4:7, 10; John 14:15). Like them, we are social beings, who need other people in our lives to encourage and exhort us in the Lord (Heb.10:24-25). How vital it is to keep the lines of communication open between ourselves and others in the faith (Psa.66:16; Mal.3:16). And our voices must be lifted up in loud praise to God (Psa.47:1, 150:1-6). This will put fear into the enemy, and he will flee (2 Chron.20:22).

Donkeys are dependent on their master for nourishment, water, shelter and protection. This applies to us too, in a physical sense as well as spiritually (Matt.6:11, 26, 31; Psa.23:2; John 6:51; 7:37-39; Psa.91). If donkeys are loaded with a burden too heavy to carry, they will valiantly try to bear it, but eventually they fall down under its weight, unable to get up until the burden is lightened. God wants to take away our load of sin, shame, guilt and fear, to replace it with His light, easy burden, which we can carry gladly and without complaint (Matt.11:28-29).

Finally, the last word is from a donkey himself. Let us not, like Balaam, be so slow to obey God that He has to use "a dumb donkey speaking with a man's voice to" restrain us in our madness and rebuke us for our iniquity (2 Pet.2:15-16– Read the whole story in Num.22:22-34).

36
CLAY POTS

The red, iron-rich clay soil in parts of Ethiopia seems particularly suited to making earthenware vessels, such as the large gourd-shaped water pots, tall coffee-makers with a long narrow neck and spout, assorted cooking pots, and huge round skillets used for cooking injera, the staple food. All are an essential part of life. Certain ethnic tribes produce these commodities, with pottery-making being the sole source of income for entire villages of subsistent farmers. Usually the potters are women, and girls begin learning the finger skills from their mother at about age six.

Typically, the molding is done by hand, without the use of a wheel. The base of the pot may be formed in a basket or leather mold, a gourd, or a hole in the ground, and clay is added as needed to form the upper part. The potter might then add decorations, which act as a trademark, before the finished product is air-dried, then polished. To produce a shiny <u>black</u> pot, it is coated with oil before firing. Most of the pots are a rusty red color. A fire is made in a pit in the ground, using hay and dried cow-dung as fuel. Several pots are fired at once, the heat sealing and strengthening the vessel. When cooled, they are taken to be sold at the local market, or shipped to buyers in other areas.

I visited a potter's village once, and watched patient, skillful hands take a shapeless lump of clay, dug out of the ground, and form it into a useful and beautiful vessel. A potter usually works in solitude, not distracted by extraneous things, but totally focused on forming the vessel already created in her mind. I like to think that our Creator did the same when He fashioned us (Isa.64:8), making each one unique, marked with His image and filled with His life (Gen.1:27; 2:7; Psa.139:14-16). We are really glorified dust, especially so if we have been redeemed by blood out of the slave market of sin, cleansed, and filled with the water of His everlasting life (John 7: 37-39; 2 Cor.4:6-7) We are just clay pots, but the treasure in us is Christ (Col.1:27), whose Spirit has sealed us as His own (Eph.4:30; 2 Cor.1:21-22), and filled us with His regenerating life, light and power, so that <u>we, the church, can manifest God's glory and wisdom to the world and to the powers of darkness!</u> (Tit.3:5; Eph.3:10) Think about these words, and ponder the depths of their truth. What an awesome privilege!

"Therefore if anyone cleanses himself . . . he will be a vessel for honor, sanctified and useful for the Master, prepared for every good work (2 Tim.2:21). "This people I have formed for Myself; They shall declare my praise" (Isa.43:21). Holy Spirit, mold me, fire me, fill me, use me!

37
THE ALUM SOLUTION

rom April to September, rains would erode the red iron-rich soil of Hosanna, Ethiopia, depositing large amounts of it in the river beds. In the ensuing months, the rusty river became a vital source of water. While the rains fell, we filled every available barrel and tank with this precious liquid. But when the dry season began, we kept that water for drinking and cooking (after boiling it for fifteen minutes!) We would hire men to haul river water (from two hours away by foot), using donkeys laden with five-gallon jerry cans or used cooking-oil containers. This murky, muddy water was poured into barrels, to be used for laundry, cleaning, and bathing.

It seems that iron floats, if it's small enough, so we sprinkled a powder called alum (aluminum sulphate) into the barrels. This amazing compound attracted the particles of iron, and carried them to the bottom of the barrel, so that murky water became clear. I just learned on the internet that this process of water-clarification and *purification* was used by the Egyptians as far back as 1400 BC. Apparently alum takes *bacteria* out of the water as well. But even with the alum, after a few months my bed sheets and other linens all turned a tell-tale rusty brown color!

I wonder at this point if my tales of life in down-country Ethiopia have made you thankful for all you have been blessed with? That is not my purpose in writing about it, but it may be a worthwhile by-product! But, I digress. Back to the lesson! Let's focus briefly on the word 'purification'. Judging by all the purification laws in the book of Numbers, it is pretty important to God. After all, He is the essence of purity, as is His Word; and He desires purity in His children (1 John 3:3; 1 Pet.1:22). But just as the pure rain picks up pollution while falling through the atmosphere, and also becomes adulterated as it flows over the earth, so do our lives become polluted with the filth on the airwaves, and corruption in the world. We become an affront to the purity of the God who lives within us (1 Cor.6:19-20), and distasteful to those who are in search of living water (1 Tim.3:7).

Our lives need continual, repeated cleansing from the impurities of our surroundings, and of our own heart, through the Word and the Holy Spirit (Eph.5:25-27; Tit.3:5; Psa.19:12, 51:2-3, 119:9), and by the blood of Christ that was shed for our cleansing (1 John 1:9). We are in the world to be a light to those walking in darkness (Matt.5:16), but the world is not to be in us (1 John 2:15-16; 2 Cor.7:1). To use another metaphor, as carriers of the water of Life, our bodies (the vessels) must be clean (1 Thes.4:4; 2 Tim.2:21), or we dishonor God, and the Gospel we represent.

"Blessed are the pure in heart, for they shall see God."
Matt.5:8

38
WARP AND WEFT

*O*n a mission station in Ethiopia, in the mid-sixties, I watched a group of students weaving, and marveled as the threads of white cotton came together with a few movements of the hands and feet of the weavers, to form a table runner, or a wall hanging, often bordered with colorful fringes. The amazing part of it was that these young weavers were blind, and depended on their teacher to make sure everything was in place, and to call on if they sensed that a thread had broken, or become tangled. They learned to trust her and rely on her to choose the pattern and provide the thread; but their lack of sight didn't keep them from doing their very best work.

The art of weaving yarn or thread into cloth has been around for several millennia, always being improved on and enhanced, but the basics remain the same. Weaving requires a loom, which simply holds the vertical warp threads in place while the filling weft/woof threads are woven horizontally through them. Before beginning to create the fabric, the weaver calculates how much thread is required and decides on the kind and color to use. He measures and cuts the required number of warp strands into equal lengths, and begins the pains-taking task of dressing or warping the loom to prepare it for weaving. (As I began writing about this, I went online to get some background information, and watched a series of videos by Elizabeth Wagner, a hand weaver and textile designer, which took me through the whole process of weaving on a floor loom. It was extremely interesting, but much too detailed to explain here.)

I have my Bible open to Psa.139, which focuses on how God knows each one of us perfectly, inside and out, and cares so much about our lives. This is because He lovingly formed us in the womb – each one unique and skillfully crafted according to His plan, and so precious to Him (vs.13-18). I get a picture of God's Spirit working at His 'loom in the womb'. He has decided the date and time of your birth, and already knows what you will look like, and what gifts He will weave into your being. And He begins, first by sparking life in you, then intricately warping the loom with threads chosen from your genealogy, to become the backdrop for the weft strands that will be woven in throughout your life. Even after you leave the womb, He will still be there to guide the shuttle as it weaves in and out. He will be there to untangle the knots and tie up the broken ends. People will marvel as they see His master-piece being perfected, and it will all happen as you present each strand of your existence to Him, and let Him perfect you, and change you into His likeness (2 Cor.3:18; Rom.12:2; Psa.138:8; Phil.1:6).

39
GUNSMOKE

I spent a few weeks one summer teaching Vacation Bible School in Jijiga, a town in Eastern Ethiopia populated by mostly Somalis. I stayed in the home of a resident missionary from Germany. One night the quiet was shattered with loud shouting, and banging. My friend came to my room, quite upset. She had identified the banging as gunshots, and could smell gun smoke in the air. She closed all the shutters, and insisted that we drag our mattresses off our beds and into the hallway, for protection against any bullets that might penetrate the outside walls. Eventually the noise subsided, and I, at least, was able to sleep.

We did not venture out in the morning, but sat tight, fearful of what the situation might be. When someone came to the door, he told us there had been a fire at one of the shops in town, and men had torn sheets of tin from the roof and sides of the building, and thrown them in a pile. . . So both the smoke and banging were explained with a few words of truth. My friend's fears were very real, but baseless. They were founded on what she had been programmed to from her past. As a young child growing up during World War II in Germany, nights filled with rifle shots, gun smoke and loud shouting were a very common occurrence. Now, what she smelled and heard had awakened in her the fear she had known more than two decades earlier.

How often do we say, "I can't—I'm afraid", bound and crippled in our lives by fear of any number of things or people? A lot of times, what we <u>fear</u> is something we think might happen, or not happen (<u>anxiety, worry</u>). One bad experience can cause long-lasting <u>phobias</u> that we never learn to overcome. Fears add up to cause <u>stress.</u> The effect of these can bring numerous emotional, mental and physical diseases and syndromes upon us to diminish our quality of life, ever increasing the fear level. See Luke 21:26.

Sometimes fears are 'caught' just by growing up with a fearful parent, and often fears are completely groundless. However they come, the good news is we don't have to be captive to them. Fear comes from our enemy, Satan (Gen.3:1-10). God's perfect love casts out fear (1 John 4:18). In place of the evil spirit of fear, God gives us His Holy Spirit, a Spirit of power, love and a sound mind (2 Tim.1:7).

- "Do not fear. . . He will come and save you." – Isa.35:4ff.
- "Fear not, for I am with you. . . I will help you" – Isa.41:10, 13
- "Do not worry. . . your . . . Father knows" – Matt.6:25-34
- "Be of good cheer! It is I; do not be afraid – Mark 6:50
- "So we may **boldly** say: 'The LORD is my helper; I will not fear. What can man do to me?'" –Heb.13:6

40
UNCAPPED SPRINGS

In rural Ethiopia, a woman may have three choices in obtaining water for her family's use. She may go to a local pond where the water is brown, contaminated, and full of parasitic worms. Or she may walk three hours to and from the nearest stream, where the water might be cleaner, but not guaranteed safe to drink. If it is the dry season, the only option may be to dig down into the sand of a dry riverbed, and wait for water to seep into the hole. In most cases the water is carried on her head in clay water pots, metal jerry cans or buckets.

Meanwhile, in many areas in the highlands, ground waters ooze out of the hills and down the slopes, some evaporating in the dry air, and some soaking into the ground to create a thin, winding green patch along its downward path. As missionaries became aware of these springs, they were able to devise a fast, cost-effective method of capping these wasted water sources, to make pure water available to the local inhabitants. It involved making a protective wall around the head of the spring, channeling the water towards a focal point where it would feed into a pipe, running the pipe through the wall and attaching a tap or several taps, where the locals could access the pure water.

Not being an engineer, I may not have accurately described this system, but the point I make is that this pure spring water was available, but for perhaps hundreds of years wasn't accessed, for lack of knowledge. Many thousands of lives were unnecessarily cut short through water-borne diseases. It reminds me of God's lament in the book of Hosea "My people are destroyed for lack of knowledge, because you have rejected knowledge" (Hos.4:6) Israel was continuously under assault by neighboring nations and finally taken in large numbers into captivity in Babylon, because they rejected the God they knew, and His ways. It wasn't that knowledge was lacking; they lacked knowledge because they refused it. When God entered history as a son of man, again the Jews rejected Him and His truth (John 1:10-11; 5:40, 43).

On so many levels, <u>we</u> are being destroyed for lack of knowledge. We muddle about in our sick, miserable existence, grumbling and complaining, stressed out and striving, longing for heaven's rest; while the living water, and the abundant life in the Spirit are ours for the taking (John 7:37-39). We reject the truths that would set us free, because they are too supernatural for our unbelieving heart to understand. We read amazing truth that never becomes reality; we reject it because it makes no sense to our natural intellect. God's Truth will set us free only if it becomes <u>our truth, and if Jesus is our life, our everything</u>! (Acts 17:28; Col.2:9-10)

41
MULES

or four years I lived on a mission station some eight thousand feet above sea level, with no roads. This necessitated the use of mules for the four-hour trek up or down the mountain. I had my own personal mule, Melinda by name, and we became quite good friends. She had her quirks, like opting to swim across a stream, rather than cross the narrow little bridge. She probably saved me from harm more than once, like the time she refused to move until the strap around her belly was tightened so the saddle wouldn't slip, and toss me off. I didn't really enjoy riding a mule, as I would quickly get saddle sore. But walking up hill at high altitudes is not easy, so when I did dismount for a break, I'd grab onto her tail, and she would help me along the steep paths!

There were other missionaries on the station, and other mules, but the pack mule was one of a kind. He would be laden with our bags, or whatever needed toting, and without reins to hold him in check, he could choose where to go. He preferred to run ahead to lead the pack. Once, on a trip home from the market, he broke away from the mule-driver, and arrived home alone, carrying his load. But he refused to let anyone near him to remove it, dodging in and out among the men chasing him.

I watched this fiasco of shouting, chasing and stone-throwing for a while, and then, on impulse, started to slowly walk towards him with my arms stretched out in front of me. Everyone stood still, as he began to approach me, half running, and then placed his sweaty head between my hands with a heaving sigh of surrender. As I spoke softly to him and stroked his face, he stood quietly, willing now to relinquish his burden.

How many of God's precious children there are who are carrying heavy burdens of responsibility and anxiety. Some are weighed down with grief, shame or guilt, so heavy they are crushed and broken. But they keep running—from judgmental voices; afraid their secrets will be discovered; overwhelmed and so, so weary.

Let the accusing voices be silent! Let the stones be dropped! Let the arms of <u>love</u> be outstretched, and words of <u>forgiveness</u> be whispered into a bruised and breaking heart (John 8:1-12). Let them hear Jesus' promise of <u>soul-rest</u> to all who come to Him and <u>lay down their burdens</u> (Matt.11:28-29). Give them words of <u>hope</u> and <u>healing</u>. Tell them of the Father's love; that He wants to <u>restore</u> their wounded spirit, soul and body in the green pastures of His Word, and <u>refresh</u> them with the still waters of His Spirit (Psalm 23). If you are the one who is running, turn and run to God, the Father who is waiting to welcome you home and lavish His love on you! (Luke 15:11-24)

42
THE WICKED FLEA

*M*other used to tell this story on her sister, my aunt. In school one day, her class was instructed to parse the sentence, "The wicked flee when no man pursueth: but the righteous are bold as a lion." (Prov.28:1–KJV). She decided that 'flee' was a noun, and 'wicked' was an adjective describing the noun. But she thought there was a mistake in the quote, because she couldn't find a verb to say what the wicked flee did!

When I went to Ethiopia, I encountered some *very* 'wicked' fleas, which had a liking for human blood, especially mine. They were ankle biters, hiding in the mud or wood floors of empty buildings, waiting to pounce on any unsuspecting human, biting repeatedly, to cause an itch that just wouldn't stop, even if you scratched your ankles raw! Calamine lotion gave only partial and temporary relief. Apparently fleas can also carry a variety of diseases, which I was fortunately not aware of at the time. Also, I was pleased to find that after several months of torture, I built up immunity to the poison they injected, and the itch was much less severe.

Unlike mosquitoes, you can't just swat and squash a flea. It is truly amazing how fast and far a flea can jump out of danger. Add to this its hard shell-like body, and you have a fight on your hands. Wetting your finger, sneaking up and pouncing on it, then tightly holding it between your thumb and finger while very carefully dissecting it with your other thumbnail, might get the job done. How can something that small be so hurtful?

Fleas remind me of offences. Offences come in many guises. For example, unkind words, such as put-downs or criticism, spoken by a parent, teacher or friend can wound and scar a child's spirit. Putting heavy responsibilities on an immature child is an offence. All kinds of abuse—physical, verbal, emotional, or sexual—are inexcusable and damaging forms of offence (Matt.18:6).

A child's spirit is so fragile, and easily crushed by offences. He (or she) may become introverted, antisocial, withdrawn. They (we) believe we are worthless, or stupid or very bad. We hide the hurt, even forgetting the events that caused these emotions and beliefs about ourselves. The spirit of offence that was allowed into our life through others becomes a part of our identity, so that even in adulthood, not only do we live with guilt and shame, but continue to receive offences (real or imagined) from people, and respond by offending others. The solution to this is to forgive our offenders, repent of the sin of offence, and cast out the spirit of offence; then <u>renew our minds by the truth of who we are in</u> Christ (2 Cor.5:17; 2 Pet.1:2-4; 1 Cor.1:30; Eph.1:3-8). Amen!

43

THE VANISHING CABBAGE

*D*uring my lunch break, I sat in a sheltered corner of the back deck, soaking up the warm rays of the tropical sun to counteract the chill of the 9,000 feet of elevation. Suddenly my eyes caught a movement in the vegetable patch, and my mouth dropped open in amazement. A head of cabbage was moving! I watched as it began to slowly disappear beneath the ground, as if pulled downward by some unseen hand. It turned out that a mole had taken up residence in the yard, digging tunnels and absconding with juicy vegetables from the garden. An excavation uncovered his cache—filled with carrots, beans, cabbage, etc., some of which was in fairly good condition! I wonder how long he would have gone undetected, if I had not caught him in the act!

I believe we can extract more than one lesson from this incident. Let's begin with where I was when the mole's thievery was perceived. Sometimes, when our hearts have become cold in the chilly air caused by lack of the oxygen of the Holy Spirit, we need to come to the shelter of God's arms, and soak in the warmth of His love. As our hearts warm to Him, we get our focus off those things that have taken us away from experiencing His love—our troubles, our illnesses, our situations. He opens our eyes to the fact that an enemy is stealing from us what *He* has given to us to enjoy—joy, peace, hope, contentment and blessings. He brings us to an "AHA" moment of revelation and discernment! (Psa.91)

What can we learn from our enemy, the mole? Just as moles live in the darkness of the underground, so our enemy, Satan, rules the kingdoms of darkness (Eph.6:12; Col.1:13). Also, like a mole, he looks for ways to make inroads into our thoughts, creating hidden tunnels of lies, accusation and deceit that can cause our lives to cave in or crumble, and we do not even know what is happening. At every opportunity, he robs us of our peace and joy, because he does not want us to live the abundant life Jesus died to give us (John 10:10).

There are other kinds of moles, none of which has a good name. Whether it is a skin mole, a cancer mole, or an espionage mole, it has a bad reputation. So what do we do when we recognize the signs that a mole is at work in our lives? Ask God's Holy Spirit to search your heart by His word, and show you where the mole of darkness has come in to destroy you (Psa.139:23-24; Heb.4:13). Repent, and receive forgiveness for allowing him in. Renounce him, and cast him out in the name of Jesus. Claim God's promise to restore, and take back what the thief has stolen from you (Luke 11:21-22). Renew your minds with the Truth so that you will be able to resist any future inroads (Rom.12:2, Eph.6:10-18).

44

MALARIA MENACE

I can remember as a child, lying in bed on hot summer nights, waiting for sleep to come, and suddenly hearing zzzzzzzzz – the familiar dreaded drone of a mosquito circling for a landing on any part of me that might provide it with a meal. I didn't mind that it might take a drop of my blood, but did it have to inject me with its venom, forming ugly welts that itched for days? I feared this tiny insect as if it were a ferocious wolf. It was such a coward, too–attacking in the dark, and putting me at a great disadvantage. My only defense was to hide under the bed sheet, and hope it wouldn't find a crack in my armor!

As I was preparing to go to Ethiopia, I was not pleased to find out that some of the mosquitoes native to that country could carry malaria, which attacks the red blood cells, causing fever and chills. Now that was adding insult to injury! The only medicine was quinine, taken in pill form. But, I learned that these malaria mosquitoes couldn't live in the rarefied air of Ethiopia's plateaus, so we would only encounter them when we took our annual holidays at a lower altitude. What a relief that I didn't have to contend with both mosquitoes *and fleas!* I conscientiously took the quinine as directed, when needed, and I praise God that I never contracted malaria! (Apparently it stays in your blood, and can recur again and again if your immune system becomes compromised).

Mosquitoes of whatever ilk are like the thoughts that come into our minds to torment us. If we allow them to land, i.e., if we listen to thoughts that are not of God, and begin to believe lies about God, about others or about ourselves, the effects on our mind and body can be devastating. But as we allow God's Spirit to renew our minds through His Word, we learn to discern where the wrong thoughts are coming from, and refuse to entertain them. God has provided His children with powerful weapons to war against the evil that assails us (Eph.6:10-18). These weapons are for "casting down arguments and every high thing that exalts itself against the knowledge of God, *bringing every thought into captivity to the obedience of Christ*" (2 Cor.10:4-6).

The Gospel of grace that we have believed is the Gospel of *Peace* (Rom.10:15; Eph.6:15), and this peace of God will "guard your hearts and minds through Christ Jesus" (Phil.4:6-9). Like a huge mosquito net it keeps out those persistent, ungodly thoughts. All your swatting, hiding and thrashing about to fend them off simply are useless. Let the "Christ in you" (Col.1:27), who by His death and resurrection triumphed over Satan and all his hosts (Col.2:13-15), continue to lead you in victory, as you yield to Him! (1 Cor.15:57)

45

THE FOURTH PLAGUE

$\mathcal{I}$ was cooking a bit of meat in a small pot on the stove, and completely forgot about it when I left for church one Sunday morning in Ethiopia. A couple of hours later, as I returned and opened the door, I was totally unprepared for what I found. Led by the odor of cooking/burning flesh, that had wafted through the cracks, and out into the air, probably every fly and his family for miles around had somehow found their way into my home! I immediately felt a twinge of sympathy for the Egyptians who were plagued with swarms of flies in their houses (Exod.8:24). It was a disgusting sight, and a daunting task lay ahead of me.

Speaking of fly families, I found out there are many varieties of flies, including some insects that aren't called flies, like gnats, and certain mosquitoes. Most of them are ugly, pesky and carriers of disease. I've met some of them, such as the house fly (no kidding!), fruit fly, black fly, horse fly, and no-see-ums; and have heard about the tsetse fly. On the other hand, some insects carry the name of 'fly' but aren't really flies, and are actually quite friendly, even attractive. They fly, but they don't act like flies. And 'fly' is part of the name, not a separate word. Some good examples are butterflies, dragonflies and fireflies. Believe it or not, there are some lessons we can learn from our friendly un-flies, and our not-so-nice real fly acquaintances!

One truth we can take from this, is that people can call you a fly, but that does not make you a fly. Really! You might have a disease, but *you are not* a disease. Maybe a parent, a teacher, or a friend, has told you that you were stupid, or you would never amount to anything; so you believed them, gave up, and just stopped trying. You fashioned your identity on lies. You became a 'fly', full of hurt, carrying toxic emotions, feeding on garbage, never rising to your true identity or your destiny in Christ. If this describes you, take heart. God is in the transforming business! When we call on Him, realizing our need for a Savior, He takes us where we are, and transforms us into His image, as His children. (Eph.2:1-10). He changes us from the inside out (2 Cor.3:17-18).

God made you with special intent, and purpose, for His praise and glory (Psa.139:14-16; Jer.29:11-13). In Christ He has provided abundant life, forgiveness of sin, wisdom and revelation, and everything you need to live like the son or daughter of a King (Eph.1:3-14; 2 Pet.1:2-4; 1 Pet.2:9). When He looks at you He sees His Son, because you are in Him, and He is in you! (Col.3:3; Gal.2:20) What He does is change you into a new creature, and gives you a new identity in Christ (2 Cor.5:17). Are you ready for a complete makeover? You will love the 'new you'!

46

MARCHING ONE BY ONE

*L*ike a chain of tiny black beads held together with invisible links, they march, swiftly and resolutely, through a crack in the mud wall, across the wooden floor, up the table leg, and straight to the prize. Today they find an almost-empty glass of sweet fruit juice, into which they swarm—some to feast, others, alas, to drown. Another day they might get into the sugar bowl—much safer—until they find themselves scooped up and into a cup of hot tea! The preferred find is a piece of sweet food, where they can eat to satiation, then carry wee morsels back home to feed their family of cute, sweet little sugar ants.

Not so cute are their much larger red cousins, who often go on marches of destruction, like an invading army, several abreast, stinging and devouring any hapless creature, small or large, that hasn't been able to get out of their path. I'm not sure if the ones who came to pay me a night visit, were a break-off group that decided to explore what lay behind the huge wall in their way; or if they were all planning to break and enter, but could only squeeze a few at a time through the fissure they located, which happened to be near the floor at the head of my bed. I woke to find them in my hair, some already stinging my scalp. I am quite calm as I write this; not so at the time. I jumped out of bed with uncharacteristic alacrity, grabbed a comb and frantically yanked it through my short locks, sending those army ants into tailspins through the air. I probably then attacked them and their buddies with bug spray, to ward them off, encouraging them to retreat and change course. Just another day in the life of a missionary!

Speaking of plundering armies: Did you know that when Satan (Lucifer) was cast out of heaven because of pride, rebellion and insurrection against God, he took one third of the angels with him—co-conspirators in his dastardly plans? (See Isa.14:12-15; Ezek.28:12-17; Rev.12:3-4a, 7-10; 2 Pet.2:4; Jude 6). In imitation of God's heavenly hosts, he formed his own army, to war in the spiritual realms against God and His people. We *are* in a warfare and the battle field is in our mind! (2 Cor.10:3-6; Rom.7:23)

Satan was defeated at the cross (Col.2:15), but he doesn't want us to know that. He knows his final end, and that his time is short to harass, accuse and bind God's people (Rev.20:10). Jesus came to destroy the works of the devil (1 John 3:8). He did this at the cross, but also in part by casting out demons and healing people of afflictions Satan had brought on them (Acts 10:38; Matt.4:23-24). And He gave us authority in His name to do the same (Matt.10:1; Mark 6:7, 12-13; 16:17-18). "The God of peace will crush Satan under your feet shortly" (Rom.16:20). Praise God!

47
HIDDEN DESTROYERS

$\mathcal{T}$ermite mounds are a common sight on the Ethiopian plains, and come in various shapes and sizes, up to two or more meters high. They rise as extensions of underground termite nests, built from within to accommodate thousands of these hungry consumers of plant fiber. A man once tried to knock over one such mound by ramming it with his truck. Result: a badly damaged truck; the termite house intact. Those structures are like petrified wood!

A termite sort of looks like a large white ant, with a mouth that resembles the business-end of pruning shears, capable of tearing wood into shreds. Eating day and night, 24/7, they devour mostly dead plant fiber, some trees, and where available, wood floors, walls and ceilings in people-houses. Once they find a way in to a structure, they set up residence and eat away incessantly at the inside of the boards, unseen, and often undetected until a hollow floor board collapses under a heavy human foot. If ignored, their destruction continues until only the varnished and painted shells of the wood remain, and the house crumbles in on itself.

To keep termites out of a house, its wood components must not contact the soil. Food sources like stumps and debris need to be removed from the yard, and gutters and vents unclogged. People who live in termite territory must keep constant vigil against these marauders. It is easier to <u>keep</u>

them out than to <u>get</u> them out once they are in. And therein is the spiritual lesson. If our mind is protected by the Word of God; cleared of junk and debris from the past, through the forgiveness and restoration of repentance; and separated from the 'dirt' of the world-system by the Holy Spirit, the termites of anger, bitterness, lust, envy, fear, pride, etc. will find no entrance, and nothing to attract them (Prov.4:20-27; Psa.119:11; 1 John 1:9; 2:15; Gal.5:16, 22-23).

Maybe you brought some termite-infested dead-wood relic from the past into the temple of God you have become (Eph.4:22-24; 1 Cor.6:19). Perhaps the termites haven't surfaced yet, but if left to proliferate, they will cause harm and destruction in your spirit, soul and body. When this starts to happen, it's a sign there is an enemy in the camp. You may not know what it is, or where it got in, but God does (Heb.4:12-13). A termite invasion wasn't His idea, and He is waiting for you to surrender your past to Him. Ask Him to show you what sins are lurking beneath the floor boards (Psa.139:23-24). Recognize and take responsibility for these sins, repent and receive His forgiveness (Psa.51:2-3). When His light shines into the deep corners of your being, those darkness-loving creepy critters will vacate the premises (1 John 1:7). Then, the light of God's Word will renew your mind and restore your soul, from the damage caused (Psa.107:20; 23:2; Josh.1:8).

48
A MENAGERIE

This book has become quite a menagerie of creatures! I haven't told you about the two-inch cockroaches I met in the desert area in Eastern Ethiopia, where I spent a few weeks one summer. Or the bedbugs in the church bench that produced a frightening hard, red welt about four inches in diameter on the back of my leg. The next time I met some of these biters, at a conference, they tormented my friend and me all night as we chased them around in our sleeping bags with flashlights. They didn't seem to bother the Ethiopian ladies who were bedded down on the hay next to us, but our antics and laughter might have! The first encounter with bedbugs a few years earlier must have acted like a vaccination, because I had no ill effects the second time!

Going up the animal chain, my zoo included spiders (in my bedroom) with fat furry bodies the size of a one-inch marble, and hairy legs and antenna to match. I soaked one such with Shelltox spray, while he stood his ground and glared defiantly at me, finally scuttling away as if I had just fed him fat flies. Hmmmm.

And what shall I say of the little lizard that hid behind a calendar in an indentation in the mud wall of my bedroom? He was quiet, harmless and kept to himself. I let him stay to catch bugs.

There were other visitors to my house that weren't so welcome. Some rats living in the mud wall around the yard decided to move into my mud-walled home. They weren't huge – about five inches long, excluding the tail. One night one such rat climbed up onto my washstand, and was eyeballing me when I opened my eyes to see what the noise was. Bravely, I got up, removed the lid from the pail of water next to the stand, and with one blow pushed him into the water, and slapped the lid on. I marveled at my courage, but felt guilty listening to him trying to escape!

Once I came upon a brilliant-green poisonous snake, his two-foot length coiled in sleep, on the outhouse floor. I retreated hastily!

I watched a cheeky brown monkey reach through the fence and pick strawberries, which he obviously enjoyed eating. In the trees nearby, large beautiful black and white Colobus monkeys swung through the treetops, feeding on juicy leaves, safe for the moment from poachers who might covet their coats for cash!

Some of the animals I didn't meet, but often in the quiet night hours on the plateaus heard the blood-curdling call, or malicious laughter of the hyena, a bone-crushing hunter and scavenger. Down on the plains it was the eerie, throaty roar of the lions that made me thankful for walled compounds, and sturdy gates.

Thank You dear Father God for Your protection and care! Psa.91.

49
MIDNIGHT VISITOR

The clinic nurse and I lived together in Ethiopia, and had hired one of the older students, Mohamed, to do chores around the house to free us up for our busy days. One day Mohamed didn't show up for work, and we learned that something had suddenly changed in this normally quiet young man. He had begun ranting and raving as if possessed, and was walking through the streets of town preaching judgment and damnation. Looking back on it I believe he was truly under the control of Satan, like the young girl possessed with a spirit of divination who followed Paul and Silas for days, crying out continuously, until an exasperated Paul commanded the evil spirit to come out of her (Acts16:16-18).

Some of the men from the church took it upon themselves to keep an eye on Mohamed, especially after dark, not sure what to do about him. They were taking a coffee break one night, when unbeknownst to them, their quarry escaped, and came to our house, reportedly to get a sharp knife in order to kill one of the school teachers. He tried the locked kitchen door, and with super-human strength snapped the quarter-inch steel door handle off. He then came to my bedroom window and punched his hand through one of the small panes of glass, cutting himself. Angered, he found a sturdy stick, and began breaking the panes and their wood frames. I woke at the sound of the shattering glass, which was flying into the room next to my bed. I jumped up, and stood against the far wall, watching, mesmerized. By this time, the nurse, having heard the commotion, grabbed her whistle, and blew it loudly, summoning the watchmen. They arrived just as Mohamed was attempting to climb through the window. I was still watching fixated, seemingly unable to move.

I wondered at the time why I was not afraid. Maybe, even then God, while protecting me, was also preparing me for the truths I have only recently learned; that we have a vicious, cruel enemy, whom we are to recognize, but not fear. The Bible teaches a lot about Satan, i.e. the devil, and his armies of evil spirits, against whom we wage an ongoing warfare (1 Pet.5:8-9; Eph.6:11-12). In Jesus' ministry, casting out evil spirits was a common occurrence (Acts 10:38; Matt.8:16). Jesus gave authority to His followers to do this as well (Matt.10:1). In His last commission, He also gave us authority to do the same (Mark 16:17; John 14:12). Yes, us!

What a tragedy that so many people are held in the clutches of Satan for years, because much of the church today has chosen to ignore the plain teaching of spiritual warfare, and our authority over the enemy of our souls, to cast him out in Jesus' name, and bring liberty to the captive! (Luke 4:16-21; 2 Tim.2:24-26).

50
ON THE HEIGHTS

My friend and I had a stopover in Lucerne, Switzerland on our way home from Ethiopia in the summer of 1968. Like most other visitors to that city, we took the train up the steepest railway in the world, to nearby Mount Pilatus. The wheels on the train were fitted with cogs that meshed with cogs in the tracks, to keep the train from slipping back when climbing, or from going too fast downhill. It truly was an unforgettable experience. To be in the Alps, enjoying the breathtaking beauty of this amazing piece of God's creation was a special privilege!

WHOA! I just saw a picture on the internet of that cogwheel train and the angle is crazy steep! I can hardly believe I was on it, and I don't remember being afraid! Maybe it's just as well we had planned to descend in the cable-car. Or maybe not! This aerial gondola was like a small bus suspended by a short cable from the long cable that stretched down into the valley below. As we boarded for the descent, a thick cloud obscured that cable, up to a few feet in front of the car. I could trust a rope I could see, but I wasn't sure about one that according to my eyes, ended in mid-air. This was way beyond driving a car in a blizzard or heavy fog. We were on top of a mountain, with a vanishing cable!

I guess it was one of those times when I had to trust what I could not see, and I may have learned a lesson in faith that day. Part way down, we transferred into smaller gondolas, and by then we had left the cloud behind, so had a wonderful bird's eye view of the panorama unfolding below.

It must be hard for those who have never stood on the top of a mountain, or flown in a small plane or helicopter, to imagine the view from the heights. Nothing has changed in the scenery, but you are seeing it from a totally new perspective. It's as if you are detached from it, and things that were huge have become barely visible. That's the way it is in God's kingdom. He wants us to live above the world, on a higher plane, our spirits soaring with Him in the heavenlies, where we are seated with Christ, <u>now</u> (Eph.2:6). Col.3:1-3 tells us we are to seek, and set our mind on things above, not on things on the earth; that our life is hidden with Christ in God, and we are dead to the things of the world.

We are not to let the cares, the encumbrances or the attractions of the world keep us from rising to our higher calling (1 John 2:15-17; Phil.3:13-14). Like the words of the old hymn, if we turn our eyes on Jesus, and look on His face, "things of earth become strangely dim in the light of His glory and grace." As we wait on the LORD, He will enable us to rise up with wings like eagles, far from the call and clamor of the world's temptations (Isa.40:31).

51
STAINS OF REBELLION

That spirit of rebellion that occasionally surfaced throughout my childhood reared its ugly head eleven years into my career as a missionary, and essentially ended it. It has been very difficult for me to even consider sharing this part of my life, because of the shame and guilt it brought. But God let me know that it is time to do so. Why? As I have ministered to women over the past few years, I have had the sense that many of them felt that I can't identify with them in their shame, because I hadn't 'been there and done that!' I would assure them that I had, but it wasn't until recently that I actually shared my story with a lady who was very hesitant to talk about her past. It was a breakthrough moment, as she opened up, was able to forgive herself, and found peace. She thanked me for making myself vulnerable, even as I do now.

I was thirty-six. And still single. I was hoping to someday find the right man, but kept having crushes on guys, and rejecting any who might begin to look interested, maybe because it wasn't *my* idea. But when a young Ethiopian fellow made it obvious that he liked me, I was flattered at first, then smitten with what I thought was real love. I broke every rule in the book, as we secretly met, sometimes not so secretly, and our relationship developed. I wanted him, and I rationalized in my mind that I deserved love!

I knew it was total rebellion, and I didn't care. I refused to heed the warnings of concerned friends, my conscience, or what I knew to be right. I rushed pell-mell down the seven-steps-to-sin that James describes in the Bible (Jas. 1:14-15). Here they are:

1. Temptation—not a sin yet. I should have stopped here.
2. Drawn away—Still not too late to turn back. I didn't.
3. My own desires—I was giving in to the lust of my heart.
4. Enticement—It looked so inviting, hard to resist.
5. Desire (lust) is conceived—And so was our baby.
6. Sin is born—My baby would be born out of wedlock.
7. Consequences—Disgrace to family, friends, the Mission.

Added to this was the utter shame, guilt and fear I felt when I realized what I had done—the same feelings Adam and Eve had after they disobeyed God. I had to tell somebody—I couldn't hide a pregnancy for long. I was so appreciative of loving people who let me vent my hurts and rebellion, and yet made plans to send me back to North America, and to discreetly dismiss me from the Mission (Gal.6:1-2). I was such a disappointment and failure. I want to apologize now to all that I let down, and that I covered it up with lies and deception. Please forgive me, as Christ has done. Only He could erase that awful sin stain! (Isa.1:18) As I prayed David's repentant words in Psa.51, like him I realized the depth of my sin, and the wonder of His restoration. What grace and mercy He lavishes on us who are so undeserving!

52
THE GRACE EXCHANGE

The wonderful friend I confided in when I realized I was pregnant arranged for me to stay with a family (friends of hers) in California, until after the baby was born. This lovely couple with two teenage girls, who did not know me, welcomed me into their home, treated me like family, and loved on me. The mother made sure I had nutritious food to nourish the child in my womb, and bought me maternity clothes and other things I needed. The parents both worked, so I did the housework, and helped out where I could. There was never a word of condemnation. The grace they showed me was unbelievably healing.

It was taken for granted that I would not keep the baby. I really had no way of caring for a child, so I didn't fight the plan. I was grateful that they arranged the adoption, and that another loving Christian couple would parent my child. Knowing what I do now, how an unwanted pregnancy and giving up a baby for adoption can have devastating consequences in the life of that child, I trust that his new parents poured love into him, so that he didn't grow up with an orphan-spirit, feeling abandoned and unwanted. And I hope that he was able to forgive me, and realize that he had a much better life than I was able to provide. My heart aches that he may have suffered in any way because of what I did.

When my temporary visa for USA expired, I had to return to face my family in Canada. I went to stay with my uncle and aunt in Alberta for about a year, and with much patience and love they helped me through my loss and pain, as I tried to deal with transitioning into a new life. (While there, I was introduced to the world of fabrics, frequently helping my aunt in her shop).

Neither they, nor my immediate family ever judged me. Maybe it was because we didn't discuss uncomfortable things. But I never *felt* judged, and was so grateful for their grace in accepting me as if nothing had ever happened. And I will never forget my oldest sister's words to me, *not to think that God was finished with me*, or that I could never have an effective ministry for Him again. Thank you, Arla, for your affirming words (1 Cor.14:3).

This morning, as I watched a program called "Hillsong" on TV, the speaker, Brian Houston, explained *God's grace* this way: "People take something glorious and ruin it; *God takes what is ruined and makes it glorious*." Jesus carried all of our disgrace on the cross. *In a Divine exchange*, His grace clothes us in righteousness. It is this grace that works in us, so that we are then able to show grace to a fallen sister or brother (2 Cor.5:21; Eph.4:29, 32; Gal.6:1). Thank You, God, for your restoring grace (Joel 2:25).

53
ADOPTED

I caught a blurry glimpse of him with my near-sighted vision, as they whisked him away, and he was gone, out of my life, adopted into a family where he would have a Christian upbringing, loving parents, brothers and sisters, and maybe a dog. It was all so final and business-like, emotionless. I had long since come to terms with the fact that I would never know this child I had felt and watched grow inside me for nine months. There were times in the beginning that I wished he would just disappear, and now he had. I promised his new Daddy and Mommy that I wouldn't try to find him, and I honored that promise for many years. When I did try, I kept hitting walls with no gates. Was he even still alive? Maybe he was killed in the Iraq War? What was his name? Had he ever tried to locate me? Did his parents tell him anything about me? Actually, I never met them. We communicated by letter, and through their lawyer. I couldn't even locate *him* years later. Maybe it was for the best. I had moved on, and was fine.

I am thankful that he had a good home, and even more thankful that I gave him life, not aborting him as was suggested to me. Why add murder to fornication? (We don't use that word much anymore, do we? But I know now, as I knew then, that it is sin.)

I love the word 'adoption'. It must take a special kind of love to choose to raise someone else's child, treat him/her as your own, lavishing them with love, care, provision and protection for the rest of your life. From day one it is a very costly commitment.

In the Bible I see a distinct difference between <u>adoption</u> and *new birth*. Both are accomplished by the Holy Spirit and the Word. But whenever mention is made of the new birth, or *being born again*, it is about *becoming citizens in the kingdom of God* (John 3:3, 5); we *receive new life, the eternal life of the Spirit* (Rom.8:9-11); we are *born into freedom in a new supernatural realm, as God's new creation* (2 Cor.5:17; 2 Pet.1:11). As kingdom dwellers, we *know and love God and other kingdom people* (1 John 4:7; 5:1); we *practice righteousness, not sin* (1 John 2:29; 3:7-9); and we *overcome the world, the kingdom of Satan* (1 John 5:4, 18).

It is <u>adoption</u> that <u>brings us into son-ship!</u> (Rom.8:15-17) We have become <u>children of God</u>, with all the <u>privileges of a son</u>, including <u>inheriting God's riches of heaven along with Jesus</u>. This was God's plan from the very beginning (Eph.1:4). Gal.4:4-7 tells us that <u>Jesus redeemed us at great cost from slavery under the law, so He could make us His sons</u>, and <u>we can call Him ABBA (Daddy) Father</u>! <u>The seal of His Spirit in us guarantees all this</u>! (2 Cor.1:20-22) How beautiful!! O, how He loves us!! (1 John 3:1-3)

54
THE FABRIC SHOP

$\mathcal{I}$ lived with my aunt and uncle for about a year, and sometimes helped my aunt in her fabric store. I remember shelves filled with hundreds of bolts of fabric, of all sorts, colors and textures. Then there were other shelves, as well as drawers and displays filled with any and every thing you might possibly need to 'sew a fine seam' – from the pins and patterns to the top-of-the-line sewing machines. I was amazed at how knowledgeable my aunt was about all these hundreds of items. What most impressed me was how she served each one of her clients with such a sweet spirit.

I can still see in my mind's eye the way she carefully and painstakingly would rewind and return to its niche each bolt of cloth, after cutting off the amount required for a dress. She would run her hand lovingly over the fabric, savoring its hues, its texture and its unique beauty. Could she envision the garment it was to become in the hands of a skilled seamstress? Was she thinking this particular fabric might not be easy to manage, and would require a lot of patience? Perhaps she was pondering the possibility that the fabric could become marred by a careless cut, spilled coffee, or an over-heated iron, and end up in the waste-basket. Was that what caused that furrow in her brow?

Each of us is like a bolt or length of fabric, made uniquely by our Creator God, who rejoices over us, and lovingly and tenderly cares for us (Zeph.3:17; Psa.91). He knows all about us, because He has put us together, marvelously and perfectly (Psa.139:13-16). We are always on His mind and in His thoughts (Psa.139:17-18); and not one of *our* thoughts or words or deeds is hidden from Him (Psa.139:1-4, 23-24; Heb.4:13). Each one of us bears the mark and image of our Creator (Gen.1:26-27), and we are made to bring glory to Him (Eph.1:4-6).

God has a plan for each one of us, which He will fulfill in us as we call on Him, and walk in His will (Jer.29:11-13). Some of us rebel and test God's patience. Others of us are marred by the many vicissitudes and wounds of life; and we are not fulfilling our God-ordained destiny. This is because we are hiding our scars and wounds, instead of coming to Him for forgiveness, cleansing and healing. God did not make you to be thrown in the trash. He is the God of second, third and a thousand chances. He is calling you to Himself today, with love, mercy and grace (Isa.1:18, 55:6-7; Matt.11:28-30; Heb.4:16). Remember that God is still in the Restoration business, changing the old into New, bringing Life to the dead, dispelling darkness with Light, giving Beauty for ashes! (2 Cor.5:17; Eph.2:10; 5:8; Isa.61:1-3) Let Him restore you today!

55
TIE-DYED TEES

ie-dying, a fashion fad that exploded onto the North American market out of the Hippie era in the late sixties brought eye-popping custom-designed psychedelic colors to T-shirts and tops, dresses, jeans and army surplus clothing. Hip young men could even purchase tie-dyed shirts and trousers!

According to Wikipedia, the custom of tie-dyeing fabrics (also known as batik) dates back to as early as 500 AD in Peru, and has also been practiced in parts of Asia and Africa for centuries. It was introduced into North America in the early nineteen hundreds. (I wonder if this procedure could have been used to make Joseph's coat of many colors!)

To explain briefly, a wet piece of cloth or clothing is folded in a pattern, and tied tightly at various places with string or elastic. Dye is applied to part of the fabric, or different sections are dipped into various colors of dye. When the fabric is untied and unfolded, voila! It has been transformed from drab to daring, from mundane to magnificent, in swirls, spirals or stripes. The original fabric shows through only at the places that were bound so tightly that the dye could not penetrate; but it is this plain background that accentuates the beauty of its transformation!

In the ho-hum and monotony of our daily lives, in the same-old, same-old dreary pattern of our days and weeks, months and years, we can get stuck in the mode of "just existing". It seems there is nothing to brighten our outlook, no hope of anything really worth living for. And then, one day, someone tells us we are loved by God (Jer.31:3; John 3:16), and He has a better plan for us, a special beautiful future and destiny, if we just come to Him (Jer.29:11-13). As we yield the fabric of our being into His hands, He washes us clean from the things of the world that have defiled us (Tit.3:5; 1 John 1:7); He lovingly folds us into new designs we never imagined (2 Cor.5:17); He binds up the places where we have been hurt and wounded (Psa.147:3; Isa.61:1-3 KJV); and He dips us again and again into the dye vats of His multi-faceted salvation until our life explodes with color, beauty and purpose (Eph.1:2-21; Col.1:9-14).

When it all unfolds we see that His love, joy, peace, patience, kindness, goodness, faithfulness, gentleness and self-control have become infused into the fibers of our being, to be displayed in the vivid hues of the Spirit's fruit for all to see (Gal.5:22-23; 2 Cor.3:18). Our lives become a living witness of God's amazing power that has transformed us by the work of His Spirit in us, revealing His glory against the backdrop of wounded, broken, and defiled lives redeemed by His grace through the death of His Son (2 Cor.4:6-7). Beautiful! Incredible! Glorious! Awesome!

56
RELINQUISHING

*W*hen I came home from Ethiopia, I decided to pack a small steamer trunk with a few things I wanted to keep. This included a set of waterless cookware, my accordion, and enough clothes to keep the pans and 'squeezebox' from banging around. I had purchased a second-hand accordion several years earlier, and taught myself to play it, with the idea that someday I would use it on the 'mission field'. It had served me well, in teaching music in school as well as playing in church services, and for the singing groups. One of the young men had shown a real interest in learning how to play the accordion, but I was very protective of it, and was not willing to either teach him or let him learn on his own with 'my' instrument. I moved on to another station, and took my precious accordion with me. So now, packing up to leave, I once again had a choice, and once more I chose to keep what I could have given away to be a blessing to others.

It was about a year before my trunk caught up to me in Canada, and when I opened it, my heart sank. The clothes had been removed at some point, leaving the other contents unprotected against any rough handling. The cookware seemed fine. But my accordion was broken–some of the reeds had become detached.

Undaunted, I purchased some glue, and set to work, having to figure out which reed went where, and then carefully reattach it. When all was back together, and I opened up the bellows, my ears were attacked with a high-pitched squeak, that wouldn't stop, and could not be drowned out by playing music. It sounded like a stuck key, but I couldn't *see* any stuck key, and had no clue how to stop the noise. I kept *my treasure* for a few more years, and finally it went out with the trash, useless and discarded.

I can't go back and change what I did. None of us can. But what I can do going forward, is hold lightly what is in my hand. Perhaps more important is my willingness to relinquish my plans, so God can fulfill His plans in me. This begins with letting go of my will, not insisting on doing things my way. Instead of saying, "God, this is what I want to do. Please bless me in it", I learn to say, "Father, take me, all of me, and fulfill Your will in me. I am the clay. You are the potter. Tune my heart to hear Your voice saying 'This is the way—walk in it'" (Rom.12:1-2; Isa.64:8; 30:21).

In God's kingdom, relinquishing includes not demanding our rights, not insisting on having our own way, not holding on to a habit or a belief or an opinion just because we don't want to change, or admit we are wrong. Often, what we are unwilling to relinquish becomes an idol, or will disappoint us or control us. Forsaking what is past, let us move on, in God's way (Phil.3:7-8).

57
NEW HORIZONS

I was over forty when I signed up to take driving lessons, and it was a major event when, at the second try, I passed the test and was issued a license to drive a car! Now I just had to find a car I could <u>afford</u>. As it turns out, I bought <u>a Ford</u>, a two-tone brown four-door Fairmont sedan, second hand. Within a few days after my purchase, I tested both the car and my driving skills by going to visit several relatives in Saskatchewan in early December—a very long drive in extremely cold, snowy weather—a woman, alone. Was I exceedingly brave or bordering on crazy?

Before I even got out of Calgary, I almost ran out of gas, because until a little red light came on, I hadn't realized I was responsible to fill the tank, if the car was to go anywhere. I skidded on the icy streets three times, just about wiping out, and also got quite lost three times. Hmm! Things didn't bode well for making it to my out-of-province destination. But my determination would not let a few glitches stand in my way, so off I went on a new adventure.

I had learned to drive in the city, and the highway speeds of 100 or 110 kilometers per hour were quite frightening. I was glad the speed limit increased gradually as I drove out of the city, so by the time I reached the outskirts I was ready to hit the gas! I was still a bit unnerved when maneuvering curves and steep hills, but loved the long stretches of straight prairie highways!

Life is constantly bringing us new challenges. These may come out of disappointments, need, or roadblocks. They can be in the form of illness or loss, marriage or a new job. If we face them, challenges will stretch and mature us. They can open up exciting new opportunities. The *secret* of dealing with the challenges we meet in life is to surrender our life to God, and not let the world squeeze us into its mold (Rom.12:1-2).

Joseph faced huge challenges, but refused to compromise. (His story unfolds in Genesis 37). The visions God gave him of his future caused jealous hatred by his brothers (vs.4-5, 8, 11). They stripped off his coat and cast him into a pit to die (v.24). He was sold to strangers for twenty shekels of silver (v.28). He was sold again in Egypt, as a slave to Potiphar (v36). **But, God was with him, giving him honor, position and authority** (Gen.39:2-5).

More challenges came. Joseph was falsely accused of rape, and thrown in jail (39:6-20). Even in his prison cell, **the LORD gave him mercy, favor, and authority.** Years later, he was released, and **his childhood dreams were fulfilled when he was set over all the land of Egypt to save lives during a seven year famine, including the lives of his brothers who now knelt before him!**

58
TRAFFIC TICKET!

*W*hen I was a fairly new driver, I was giving a friend a ride home after the evening church service. I had dropped her off, and was stopped at a red light, waiting to make a left turn. The minivan in front of me executed the turn, and I followed, eyes on the road. **CRUNCH!!!** A huge car had crashed into my little one, and I could hear bits of metal dropping onto the pavement. I burst into tears of embarrassment as a young man approached my car window, to make sure I was all right. I started to apologize, but he assured me it was okay, as long as I wasn't hurt. I got out to survey the damages. The V-shaped stainless steel nose of his car had made a serious impact on my grill and bumper, and radiator fluid was making a dark, slippery puddle on the road, *in the intersection*!

As we waited for the police to arrive, this man kept reassuring me. He, too, was on his way home from church with his mother, and they were both unharmed, as was his car. After the police assessed the scene, he was able to drive off, and a tow-truck was called to tow my disabled 'chariot' to the auto-body shop. Meanwhile, I was issued the inevitable traffic ticket, fifty dollars, for what they called an 'unsafe left turn'. Later I faced the thousand-dollar repair bill, plus a sizable increase in insurance premiums. I am much more careful making left turns now!

Have you ever made any embarrassing and costly 'left turns'? Sometimes in life, even when we seem to have a go-ahead green light, we do not always have the right-of-way! It may also be that we don't realize the potential harmful result of turning off the road we are on. To avoid collision we must be constantly alert and aware of where we are, and of the possible dangers around us, without being paranoid and fearful. (1 Pet.5:8 – "Be sober, be vigilant; because your adversary the devil walks about like a roaring lion"; Eph.5:15 – "Walk circumspectly, not as fools, but as wise"; Jas.1:5 – God will give you wisdom – just ask Him)

Wouldn't it be nice if we had an inner voice telling us where to go and what to do, so we wouldn't get into bad situations, which we regret forever? According to The Bible, we do! Maybe <u>we just don't listen, or can't hear because of all the noise in our life</u>. God speaks to us through His Spirit in us, in a voice, dream, vision, or even just a knowing in our spirit, showing us which road to take. As you read His Word, start listening for His voice. Get rid of the clutter that drowns it out, and walk in a plain path! See 1 Kings 19:12-13 – "a still, small voice"; Isa.30:21 – "Your ears shall hear a word behind you, saying, 'This is the way, walk in it'"; Acts 18:9 – "The Lord spoke to Paul in a vision" ; Matt.2:22 – Joseph was "warned by God in a dream"; John 10:4 – "The sheep follow Him, for they know His voice"; John 19:37 – "Everyone who is of the truth hears My voice". Are *you* tuned in?

59
CURB CRUNCH

'It was a dark and stormy night, and the rain came down in torrents', as I drove my little Ford Fairmont home from a friend's place. The street lights reflecting off the wet pavement greatly reduced visibility as I turned onto the main road through the city centre. Too late I realized I was in the right-turn lane. Directly in front of me was a triangular curb, complete with sign. Somehow I missed the sign, but <u>bounced</u> onto and over the curb, across the intersecting street, then over a matching curb triangle on the other side, landing hard on the road—and kept going. Something seemed to be wrong with the steering, and I was thinking I had really wrecked the wheel alignment. Coaxing and wrestling my traumatized car the final 15 or so kilometers home, I inspected the damages. The right front tire was extremely flat, which was no surprise. I had a spare, so decided to change it in the morning.

The next day was Sunday, and I wanted to go to church. As I was getting ready to change the tire, I noticed the hub-cap was missing. At least I didn't have to remove it! But loosening the lug nuts was beyond my strength, so I called the Motor Association. As I waited for them to arrive, I circled the car to check for other signs of damage. Everything seemed fine, except that not just one, but all four hubcaps had vanished. I started to laugh at the picture I got in my mind of those shiny discs bouncing and rolling along that stretch of road in the rain! I wonder where they ended up. I never replaced them, right up to the day someone hit me from behind, and I bade farewell to my battered friend.

If my car could have talked, what might it have said? Its tale could reflect the story of many people, maybe yours. Life starts out okay—you're brand new, beautiful, admired and pampered. But often, as the days and years pass, those who once cared lovingly for you may start to abuse you. No matter how hard you try to please, it's never enough, and the damage begins to show in your spirit. You are the brunt of their anger; you are hurt by their wrong behavior and their bad decisions. You begin to feel ugly, unwanted, rejected, and worthless. As the cruelties of life shake your whole psyche, you watch your self-respect roll off into the darkness that envelops your soul. You have no hope.

But you are not a machine—you are a beautiful person made in the image of God. And He wants to restore you to that amazing creature He planned you to be. Come to Him, with all your hurts, your hopelessness, and your helplessness. Give them to Him and let Him heal you. Ask Him to fill you with His love, peace and joy. This is your inheritance as His child. It was for this reason that Jesus died. Let His Spirit in you erase the past and give you a new abundant life! (Isa.61:1-3; John 10:10; 2 Cor.5:17; Jer.29:11-13)

60
GET DOWN!

was standing at the side counter, in the bank where I was employed. The girl beside me was new, and I was showing her the ropes. A man approached the counter, dressed in a trench coat, fedora, and dark glasses. He was carrying an umbrella, which he placed on the counter. He tossed a draw-string bag across the divider to a teller, and slapped a piece of brown paper covered with large printing, on the counter in front of me. It read: "Fill the bag with all your large bills, and be quick about it." I glanced at his umbrella — it was a sawed-off shot gun! He swung it around and ordered all the customers to "Get down on the floor, and don't move!" They obeyed! My fellow worker was frozen with fright, so I picked up the hold-up note, and went to help the teller fill the robber's bag. He impatiently yanked it from her. I stepped back, and watched as he backed up towards the door. Suddenly he pointed his gun at me, and hissed "GET DOWN!" I joined the other employees hunched behind the teller wickets.

Our bank was close to an army base, and there were a few young uniformed soldiers in the customer line-up. As soon as the robber went through the door, one soldier stood up and started chase, but quickly backed off when lead shot from the robber's gun hit the ground at his feet!

In John 10:10 Jesus refers to Satan as "the thief" that "does not come except to <u>steal</u>, and to <u>kill</u>, and to <u>destroy</u>". That is his purpose, and his agenda. He is at total counter-purposes with God's plan to give us the abundant life which Jesus died to make possible. He often comes in disguise, so we won't recognize who he is, and slam the door before he can enter. He doesn't usually appear with blazing pistols to take us out—he knows that if he kills our body, we will go to be with our dear Savior, and he could get no pleasure out of tormenting us. He uses strategy and tactics to infiltrate God's church and His people with lies, doubts, fears, occultic practices, unholy living, depression, addictions, etc., until we accept these things as the norm. What a travesty!

One of the first things we need to do to ward off this destroying enemy is to realize he is real, active and at work in the world and among God's people today. We are not doing ourselves a favor by denying his existence (1 Pet.5:8).

At the same time we must guard our minds and hearts with God's Word and His Spirit, so that he cannot penetrate the armor God has given us to stand against him. The One within us as God's people is greater than this enemy (1 John 4:4). As we follow the voice of the Shepherd, we will not listen to the voice of the robber (John 10:4-5). And we have the authority of Jesus' name to cast him out (Luke 10:17-19; Mark 16:17-18).

61
A TANGLED WEB

*A*fter I left Ethiopia I still kept in touch with the baby's father, and we continued to make plans for him to come to Canada. The new Communist government in Ethiopia wasn't making it easy. He was told that if he was married to a Canadian, he could get an exit visa. As soon as I got a job and earned enough money for the trip, I went back and we were married in a civil ceremony the day before I flew home. Soon after, he was conscripted into the army, for a minimum of two years. The years dragged on, and I made a couple more visits. I could see changes in him, that I didn't like, but I was committed for the long haul. Finally, my husband had had enough, walked across the border into Kenya, and spent some time in a refugee camp. With the help of the Red Cross and the Canadian Embassy, a landed immigrant visa for Canada was procured, and we were united after thirteen years.

Everything was great, at first. He got a job, his driver's license, and Canadian citizenship. But he became more and more distant, controlling, unwilling to help with expenses, accusing me of infidelity. I was broken-hearted, felt used and betrayed, crying buckets of tears. When the mental abuse turned physical, I leased an apartment and left, with a few household items.

I knew he wanted me to divorce him, but I refused. I wasn't about to add to my list of disgraces. We actually tried getting together again for a while, but I could see that there had been no real change in him. (What did I expect?) I lived in limbo, gradually letting go of the past, burning the letters he had written through all those years, etc. Five years after I left, he filed for divorce, at the insistence of his new girl-friend. I signed the papers, relieved and yet feeling rejected and forsaken.

Once again, during this period of my life, I had a loving church family who stood by me. I hadn't ever told anyone about the baby, not seeing that there was a need for them to know. To use the famous words of Sir Walter Scott in his epic poem 'Marmion': "O, what a tangled web we weave, when first we practice to deceive." And then there are those oft-quoted words from Gal. 6:7: "Do not be deceived, God is not mocked; for whatever a man/*woman* sows, that he/*she* will also reap." I knew that I had certainly deserved all the unpleasant con-sequences of my sin, and really had only myself to blame. I didn't know how long that tangled web would keep me bound in its sticky strands. In my previous book, "He Brought Me Out", I wrote about the journey that took me out of the bondage of the past, into the freedom of forgiveness and restoration (Psa.40:2-3). Praise God!

62
PATCHWORK QUILTS

*A*re you old enough to remember the Fortrel fashion phase of the 1960's? It was polyester gone wild, like the rest of western culture of that time. There were new, bright colors, like a pond full of exotic tropical fish. And the textures were endless—made by (?) some sort of huge embossed printing press that through heat and force created a raised pattern on the surface of the cloth. It was like leather-tooling, or metal-etching or monograms on paper, now in a whole new medium. Another feature of this amazing material is that it was practically indestructible with normal wear. It wasn't a good idea to get too close to a fire, as it was prone to melting and shriveling up as most plastics would.

After all the children left home, my mother took up quilting. She had stored up her old fortrel dresses, and other pieces of cloth, which she cut into squares and sewed together in designs for the quilts she made for her grandchildren. Each one was a labor of love that provided warmth and pleasure, and a reminder of times gone by. When Mom passed on, we gave her quilting frame and patches to her good friend and neighbor, who had been her home-care 'nurse' for some time. This dear woman created a beautiful quilt in memory of my mother, a keepsake fashioned from the colorful fabric of her life on this earth.

My mother's journey was by no means easy. She was trained as a teacher, but her family became her pupils, and her home the classroom. Her duties included cooking for her family, tirelessly jarring fruit, vegetables and meat throughout the summer to sustain us through the winter. Lunches were packed for school on the farm, and in town there was always a hearty meal ready when we walked home for lunch. Then there was the endless laundry, ironing and cleaning. When needed, she purchased our clothing, as well as birthday and Christmas gifts through mail-order catalogues. Those were truly the good old days!

My mother knew who she was, and was proud of her children. She loved, honored and respected my father, because she knew he dearly loved her. I believe it was this love, and her heavenly Father's love that sustained her through every circumstance of life, even when Daddy began to display signs of dementia, and passed away after their forty-six years of marriage. She carried on for another sixteen years in her cottage home, before joining him and their precious Ella May in the Father's house. She didn't receive any medal for bravery on this earth, but I'm sure the smile from her Savior, and His words of approval were ample reward and recognition for her faithfulness and courage. (See John 14:1-6; Matt.25:21; Jas.1:12). I anticipate the final family reunion, when we will be forever with the Lord! (1 Thes.4:17)

63
FABRICATION

I only just realized that the word 'fabrication' is a legitimate word used to cover the processes of putting things together to make or manufacture an article, including fabric. I had thought it exclusively meant 'an untruthful statement'; 'fraudulent or false information' (Wikipedia) or a tall tale. It seems the word comes up a lot in the courts of law, at police check-points, or in any instance where a person is trying to wiggle out of trouble. It is also used for those who deceive people into doing something which benefits the fabricator, but is detrimental to the victim.

My older brother loved to regale us with fabricated stories such as the one about the Queen inspecting the troops when he was serving in the army. According to him, he greeted her with a casual "Hi, Liz! How are you doing?", and she responded in kind. I didn't realize how convincing he really sounded until one of my cousins said to me at my Mother's funeral reception, "Wow, your mother was some special woman." I knew immediately what she was referring to, and had to burst the bubble. I had heard Dave recount how Mom was out in the field stooking sheaves of grain when she went into labor with him. She stopped stooking long enough to give birth, then laid him in the shade of a stook, took up her pitch fork and resumed working. It was a total fabrication!

In the bad sense of the word, the greatest fabricator of all time is without doubt the one Jesus called "a liar, and the father of it". (John 8:44). He enters the scene of man in Gen.3:1-5, and exits in Rev.20:10. In the Garden of Eden the serpent had deceived Eve into eating the forbidden fruit. by twisting the truth of God into a lie, saying that God was really holding back the knowledge of good and evil from them, by threatening death, and they really wouldn't die if they ate the fruit. Suddenly Eve and her husband (who also ate) became aware of evil, and were filled with fear, guilt and shame. They were separated from God by their sin (a spiritual death worse by far than the separation of soul and body which would come later in physical death).

Satan still lives up to his reputation, big time. Ponder the solemn truths of these scriptures, and see how he deceives us by his lies.

- 2 Cor.11:3—minds corrupted with a false gospel
- 2 Tim.3:13—rise of evil men and imposters
- 2 Pet.2:1-3—destructive, exploiting heresies
- Eph.5:3-7; Gal.6:7—deceived into ungodly living
- Matt.24:24—deceiving the church by signs and wonders

Eph.6:10-18 outlines our protection against Satan's deceit. If we know the truth, we will discern the lies and deception!

64
ABOUT SPROUTS

A certain woman, desiring to benefit from the nutrition of 'live' foods, went out to the market place and purchased mung bean seeds, and special sieve-like lids for sprouting-jars. (The <u>jars</u> weren't sprouting – they were the receptacles for sprouting the seeds). Having measured out about a third of a cup of seeds, she placed them in a quart jar, screwed on the lid, and ran warm tap water through the lid, to cover the seeds, and let them soak for twelve hours. The water was then drained off the now softer, swollen seeds; they were rinsed, and the jar laid on its side on her kitchen counter where she could watch these hard little green 'pebbles' come alive. Two or three times a day, she rinsed the seeds with fresh water. Soon tiny white shoots appeared on some of the seeds. Life had been awakened, and green leaves followed. After just a few days, the jar was full of crispy bean sprouts, bursting with healthy enzymes and vitamins, to be used in salads, stir fries or Egg Foo Yong. Yum!

But it came to pass one day, as she was relishing their goodness, that she bit down on a hard, un-sprouted seed that was hidden among the sprouts. She cried out in fear for her traumatized molars. In one split second, her pleasure was turned into pain. Nonetheless, she did not give up growing and eating bean sprouts, instead learning lessons through the experience.

What is the meaning of this parable?

- The hard seed is like the unregenerate heart of man (i.e. mankind) (Mark 3:5, Zech.7:12).
- The water represents the Holy Spirit, who through the Word of God, works in a hard heart to soften it, and awaken it to new life in the Spirit (Ezek.11:19-20; John 6:63; Rom.8:10-11; Gal.4:6).
- The seeds that sprout are like the hearts of people awakened to live out their purpose to glorify God and bless others (Eph.2:1-10).
- The un-sprouted seed is a picture of the heart of one who rejects the message of life, and refuses to repent, believe, embrace and live out the truth of new life in Christ Jesus (Rom.2:4-5). It may continue to hang out with the living sprouts, pretending to be a sprout, but actually may just give sprouts a bad name in the world.

Let the one with ears to hear take heed to the lesson the sprouts can teach us about the Kingdom of God!

65
OUCH!!

*Q*uite by accident the woman in the preceding parable discovered a pretty-much foolproof way to avoid broken teeth due to un-sprouted seeds. These days, the jar containing the mung bean seeds is filled to the brim with the *hottest* tap water, and left to cool. In four hours or so, the water is drained off, and the seeds are subjected to another blast of scalding water, covering them to about an inch above the beans! If they could feel, and talk, no doubt they would be complaining loudly about this cruel thing happening to them. But, in about eight hours, every seed shows evidence of new life!

It seems some seeds are so hard, that the only thing able to crack their tough exterior is heat. At the same time, the wet heat accelerates the growth process, so within two to two and a half days the jar is packed full with sprouted goodness!

I am reminded of two common idioms: "a tough nut to crack" and "turn the heat up". In the case of bean sprouts, and of people, turning the heat up, i.e. bringing some extra pressure to bear, may be the only way to crack the nut! For Saul, it took a blinding light from heaven, which prostrated him; the rebuke of the risen, ascended Lord; three days without food or water; and the filling of the Holy Spirit, for the scales to fall from his eyes. Before the heat was turned up, he was on a mission from hell to destroy the Christ-followers. But God had a plan for him—to become a believer in Christ, and to bring the Gospel of salvation to his fellow Jews, and expressly to non-Jews (Gentiles) (Acts 9).

The Old Testament record is replete with examples of Israel's disobedience to God, turning away from Him to worship the idols of the Gentiles. In order to save them from themselves and their wickedness, God would let them taste life under cruel bondage to other nations, until they repented of their sins and cried out to Him to save them. The whole of Psalm 78 is given to accounts of God's kindness and mercy to His repeatedly rebellious people.

Many a mother has prayed for years for her wayward child to come back to God. Often that one has to "come to the end of his rope", facing extreme hardship, pain, even imminent death, before, like the prodigal son of Luke 15:11-24, he is ready to come home to the Father, and enjoy the abundance of His riches.

It is not God's intention to hurt His children, but if we are willfully disobedient, and trusting others instead of Him, He may allow trials to come, to bring us to repentance of sin and unbelief. It is in the fire of testing that our faith (and our heart) is purified like gold (Job 23:10; Jas.1:2-3; 1 Pet.1:6-7; 2 Cor.4:17).

66
SPROUTS AGAIN??

Sprouts have been a part of the fabric of my life for years – in fact I eat some almost every day. And for the purpose of this book, we will learn yet another lesson from the sprout jar. Please humor me one more time!

I have found that when the life in a seed is awakened, it first sends out a root, seeking for a place to anchor itself, preferably in a rich soil where it will receive nourishment in order to grow to maturity. As a new believer in Christ, we need the nourishment of the Word of God, watered by the Holy Spirit. The new life in us seeks this, but if we do not find it, or if we choose not to hear and understand the Word, we will wither, dry up and never reach our purpose in God's kingdom. (Now would be a good time to read Jesus' parable of the sower and the seed in Matt.13:3-9, 18-23). I Pet.2:2 tells us we are like new-born babies, who need to go after the milk of the Word, so we will grow! Jesus said that we live (are nourished, grow and mature) "by every word that proceeds from the mouth of God". The Word of God anchors us, feeds us and grows us (2 Tim.3:15-17). Jas.1:21-25 says we will be blessed as we not just hear the Word but are doers of it. Let the Holy Spirit guide you into His truth (John 16:13), and transform you into the image of Christ! (2 Cor.3:18)

Back to the sprouts! As the root grows downward, a stem, crowned with a leaf or two, emerges from deep inside the seed, pushing out and upward, seeking the sun. As the light caresses those tiny leaves, they receive energy for their new life, become green, and give off life-giving oxygen—an amazing picture of our new life in Christ! (Psa.1:2-3; 92:12-14; Jer.17:7-8; John 6:63)

BUT, we have a problem! The old seed-coat that was so hard to crack, is no longer needed, and, in fact, is dead. Before the leaves appear, these husks must be flushed out with running water, or they will putrefy and spoil the sprouts. Often as a root starts to grow, it pierces the husk, and hangs on to it. We, too, may cling to the ways of the old life, dead works or besetting sins of the fleshly nature, so the Holy Spirit can't flush them out of our life (Heb.12:1; Eph.4:31; Col.3:8). It requires time and diligence to extricate these old husks from our lives, and it may be painful, but they need to be dealt with or the results are deadly. This is the process of sanctification (2 Tim.2:21). Our part in this is:

1) repenting of and receiving forgiveness for entertaining spirits of bitterness, anger, unbelief, pride, fear, and lust, etc.
2) refuting and renouncing them (2 Cor.4:2; Eph.4:22-23)
3) casting them out in the name of Jesus.

Let's keep God's temple pure! (1 Cor.6:19-20; 2 Cor.7:1)

67
SKATEBOARDING

was babysitting two-year-old Joel, while his parents and older siblings were at Kids' Clubs at church. Joel decided we should skateboard. So he got his brother's board and we headed out to the paved street which formed a cul-de-sac in front of their house. He explained that he would stand with both feet on the board, and I was to run along-side, holding onto his upraised hands. It actually worked, but I was the only one getting any exercise! Suddenly, the wheels of the skateboard hit something on the road and it abruptly stopped. The momentum of our great speed pro-pelled us both forward, and ground-ward, while the board tipped, then fell over behind us.

I was still holding tightly on to Joel's hands, but realized on the way down that if I continued on this course I would land on top of him and squash him. So I lunged to the side, smashing into the asphalt with my face and left shoulder. **Crunch!** My glasses were bent, but not broken. My shoulder, however, felt very much broken. Joel was crying, and when I asked him if he was all right he wailed "N-o-o." Dragging myself to my feet, I picked him and the skateboard up with my right arm, and we called the party off! Neither one of us was in the mood for more fun. Back in the house, I checked Joel out, and applied a Band-aid to his scraped hand. *His* crying was over, but not *mine*!

I sat on the couch and moaned with pain, while he sat very quietly next to me, full of sympathy, but unable to help. When the family returned, I drove to the hospital and waited for X-rays, which showed that my collar bone was broken right at the shoulder. A sling eased the pain, and I managed to drive home. In a few weeks I regained full use of my shoulder and have never had any residual trouble with it. How amazingly we are created!

The following Sunday, the Pastor sort of announced in church that I had broken my collar-bone skateboarding. It made a good story—I was in my mid-sixties! The thing is, it was only partly true. Neither Joel nor I was really skateboarding. We were faking it, and everything was fun, until we hit the bump in the road.

Have you ever been brought up short by an unexpected, tragic event in your normally smooth life? Did fear grip you as you felt yourself going down? Then the pain set in, but you had to ignore it, be strong for your family. Maybe years have gone by, and inside, the unexpressed grief has left you in a perpetual state of sadness, depression, and maybe chronic physical illness. Bring your grief to God right now, and pour out your sorrow to Him, with a flood of those pent-up tears (Isa.53:4-5). Receive not just His comfort, but His healing, restoration and joy! (Isa.61:1-3)

68
CRUISING DOWN THE RIVER

*I*t was quite hilarious really. Not to be outdone by the men and boys, a group of gals from our church was about to embark on a canoe and rafting trip down the Red Deer River (We did have a few men along). The guys had enjoyed a wonderful trip on a previous week-end, with gorgeous weather, so we were excited. That sort of ebbed when clouds gathered, and we had to open umbrellas and don rain ponchos, as a steady drizzle set in. Our trip took us through the badlands, with hoodoos and other strange rock formations on the steep river banks. Vegetation was sparse, as was wildlife. When there was a lull in our chatter, the silence was eerie, especially when we joined our canoes, and just floated. A lone blue heron, like a guide and sentinel, kept flying ahead, then waiting for us on the shore, standing tall and still.

My skill with a paddle was sadly deficient, so my craft kept going sideways, and in circles — funny to watch, but very frustrating for those wanting to make forward progress. It worked better when I watched as someone else paddled! We made it through the first day, then set up tents on the shore, ate and slept. The next day was sunny and warm, and by early afternoon we reached our pick-up point and were transported home. What an experience!

Remember the autograph albums from bygone days? I had one for my friends to write messages in, and a favorite notation was "Love many. Trust few. Always paddle your own canoe". There is *some* good advice here, i.e. you would like to trust people, but many just aren't trustworthy. Also, in truth, we are ultimately responsible for our own lives, and most of us don't appreciate it when others try to run (ruin?) our lives. But what do you do when your life goes sideways, or you keep going in circles, marking time, getting nowhere? What happens when things get out of control? At the least you need caring people, who can teach, train, help, maybe even bail you out (Gal.6:2; Isa.58:6-7, 10; 1 Thes.5:14).

It can be daunting to paddle your own canoe. Taking the reins and charting the course of your *life* can be *terrifying*, and end up in destruction by fear, stress and anxiety. This was never God's will for you. In love He has planned your destiny, and calls you to come to Him through Jesus to receive full, abundant life, guided and empowered by His Spirit (Jer.29:11-13; Rom.8:11, 12:1; John 10:10b; Psa.32:8; 2 Pet.1:2-4). Don't learn the hard way, by "doing things *your* way", and ignoring *God's* way. Every one professing to follow Him, needs to relinquish control to "the Shepherd and Overseer of your souls" (1 Pet.2:25). Do it today!

69
A NEW PERSPECTIVE

The last twenty-eight years of my pre-retirement life were spent in the banking world. When I started, I had no clue, but in the end I at least knew the difference between a debit and a credit, and that black stood for debits, and red for credits. For a bank, a credit (red) is a good thing, because money is coming in. Debits (black) mean money is going out, not a good thing.

After retirement I decided to take some accounting courses, including a QuickBooks course in computer accounting. When I began with the basics, I was very confused, and kept asking the teacher questions about debits and credits. Finally, she asked me, "Have you worked in a bank?" How did she know? Turns out, what is true for the bank is not true for the customer, and vice versa; and accountants work mostly with customers. The mystery was solved, as I now saw that if my account is in the black, that's good for me—it means I have money in the bank. Red means I have spent too much money from my account, and am thus in an overdraft position (punished with interest charges!). The way I looked at the red and black factor of finances depended on my perspective. But after twenty-eight years of learning one way, it was not easy to switch gears. Frankly, I'm still confused at times!

Most of us have been programmed for years to believe certain things, including the lies of our spiritual enemy, Satan.

It may be his words through parents or teachers, which have programmed us to believe we are worthless, stupid or ugly. The thought pathways in our brain have been worn into deep ruts as we have gone over and over these lies in our thinking. So when we realize, by the grace of God, that we are loved, valued and cherished by God Himself, our whole perspective changes. It is time to trace new pathways in our mind, with the truth of God. This process is called renewal of the mind (Eph.4:21-24; Col.3:10; Rom.12:2).

Just as habits are formed by repetition, our minds are renewed by the Spirit of God, as we continuously repeat and believe God's truth. Say it – <u>I am His beloved child</u> (I John 3:1); <u>He rejoices over me</u> (Zeph.3:17); <u>He has a plan for my life</u> (Jer.29:11-13); <u>He forgives all my iniquities and heals all my diseases</u> (Psa.103:2-5); <u>I can trust Him fully</u> (Psa.34:5-8; Rom.8:31-39; Heb.13:5-6); <u>He lives in me by His Spirit to give me an amazing new life here on this earth</u> (Rom.8:2, 10-11; 2 Pet.1:2-4); and <u>I have a wonderful future with Him in heaven</u> (1 Cor.2:9; Eph.2:4-7).

As these new pathways of truth are laid down in your mind, the old pathways of lies are cancelled and forgotten (Eph.4:23-24; Col.3:12-16; Tit.3:3-6). You now walk in new life! (2 Cor.5:17)

70
CATARACTS

*A*few years ago, when my optometrist detected a sign of the beginning of cataracts in my eyes, and recommended taking Lutein to slow their development, I wasn't exactly thrilled. A year later, he set up an appointment for me with an eye surgeon, even though I had no noticeable evidence of a problem. Frankly, I was glad he didn't wait until my sight was affected. A cataract is a condition in which, with advancing age, the crystalline lens of the eye stiffens and hardens, making it more difficult to focus. Using microsurgery, the natural lens is removed, and replaced with what they call an intraocular lens. After consultation, I opted for a 'Crystalens' which would allow me to see well at any distance, without glasses. Yeah! No more glasses!

The surgery was quick and relatively painless, and I dutifully did the eye-patch, eye-drops, dark goggle routine, then the exercises (daily Word-find puzzles of diminishing size for three weeks). But in the end, things were still fuzzy around the edges, and I was told it was astigmatism, and that I would need reading glasses. Whoa! I wasn't told about that! "Well", the doctor said, "I can easily correct it with laser surgery, but that will cost you extra." I did have a job, so I agreed, and the blurring was eradicated.

Eyes are extremely important, and amazing parts of our bodies! They are referenced about six hundred times in the Bible. Here are a few verses for your contemplation:

- "Everyone did what was right in his own eyes." Judg.17:6
- "The eyes of the LORD run to and fro throughout the whole earth, to show Himself strong on behalf of those whose heart is loyal to Him." 2 Chron.16:9
- "The eyes of the LORD are on the righteous." Psa.34:15
- "I will set nothing wicked before my eyes." Psa.101:3
- "I will instruct you. . . I will guide you with My eye." Psa.32:8
- "My eyes are upon You, O GOD the Lord." Psa.141:8
- "Do not be wise in your own eyes." Prov.3:7
- "The eyes of the blind shall be opened." Isa.35:5, 29:18
- "Why do you look at the speck in your brother's eye, but do not consider the plank in your own eye?" Matt.7:3
- "Lift up your eyes and look at the fields, for they are already white for harvest!" John 4:35
- "Their eyes were opened and they knew Him." Luke 24:31
- "I send you to open their eyes, to turn them from darkness to light, from the power of Satan to God." Acts 26:17-18
- "the eyes of your understanding being enlightened, that you may know. . . the working of His mighty power." Eph.1:18-19
- "God will wipe every tear from their eyes." Rev.21:4

71
THE "C" WORD

*O*n my Mother's mind, you didn't talk about certain things. So we heard about her surgery for colon cancer only after it was over. I suppose she wanted us not to be worried about her. She lived for quite a few years post-cancer, but finally succumbed as it spread to other parts of her body. I was somewhere in the same age-range, when tests confirmed that I, too, had a cancerous tumor the size of a plum in the sigmoid area of my colon. It had already gone through the wall of the colon, and into the surrounding lymph nodes. I went into surgery with the support and prayers of family members and church friends. A laparoscopic procedure was used to remove a foot of colon, with very little scarring or pain, and I was soon up and about and back to work. Praise God for a good surgeon! I told people that I now have a semi-colon!

I was pressured to have follow-up chemo, but declined. My regular Doctor had said he would help me build up my immune system with supplements, as well as a diet change; and regular tests have consistently shown no advancement over the last five years. I believe God has healed me, but I also believe there was a reason why my colon was a prime target for cancer. Since my surgery I have learned that the cause of many diseases and syndromes can be traced to spiritual roots, such as fear, anxiety, guilt, shame, occult practices, un-forgiveness, anger, bitterness, and trauma from abuse or neglect, often carried from one generation to another. In researching the roots of colon cancer, the Holy Spirit showed me that I needed to repent for myself and my generations, of the sin of slander with the tongue, a critical spirit, and accusation against myself, others and/or God. I realized that these things that I had participated in were as ugly and deadly as cancer is. Cancer was a reflection in my body of the blights on my soul. With this insight, I took responsibility, repented of and renounced them, and cast them out in the name of Jesus. Healing is a natural result of soul-cleansing, forgiveness, and restoration to fellowship with God. The subsequent peace in spirit, mind and body, causes the body to function the way it was meant to do. As Paul wrote "May the God of peace Himself *sanctify you completely*; and may your whole spirit, soul and body be preserved blameless at the coming of our Lord Jesus Christ." (I Thes.5:23; Isa.53:5; 1 Pet.2:24; Psa.103:2-5; 3 John 2).

In 2 Cor.6:14-18, Paul pleads with believers to live holy lives; in the opening verse of chapter seven, he adds, "let us cleanse ourselves from all filthiness of the flesh and spirit. . . " A good place to start is to pray the words of Psa.139:23-24 and Psa.51 from a sincere heart, and acknowledge and repent of what He shows you that is keeping you from His blessing and health.

72
LIFE IN THE BLOOD

My Dad was a very giving person. So it was only natural that he would donate blood to the Red Cross whenever he could, and encouraged me as a young adult to do the same. I did so any chance I had. It's amazing that a transfusion of a person's blood into the veins of someone else who has lost blood through trauma, infuses new life and energy into the receiver.

I was fascinated in school by a study of the circulatory system. As I understand it, the pumping of the heart forces oxygen-laden blood fresh from the lungs out into the arteries, and it flows through the body, delivering oxygen and nutrients to the tissues. By the time the blood reaches the extremities the arteries have divided into many tiny capillaries, and now the blood flows back to the heart through the veins, this time in a steady stream. On this return journey, the blood collects impurities and carbon dioxide waste (produced by the burning of food for energy) from the tissues, so the blood becomes dark in color. Donated blood is taken from a vein, so is not pure, but still carries life (Lev.17:11). (This is a lesson in itself—we don't have to be perfectly sinless to _carry_ the life *of the Spirit to those waiting to receive it!*)

When the heart receives back the 'impure' blood, it ships it off to the lungs for 'cleaning'. The lungs extract the carbon dioxide and other waste, and exhale it, exchanging it with the oxygen they have inhaled. This purified blood is then sent back to the heart. What a beautiful picture of the great exchange God makes in our lives, through the precious blood of His Son. The blood that gushed from Jesus' side was straight from His heart—pure blood that infuses life into each of us. It nourishes us, and removes the sin impurities from us (1 John 1:7). Jesus' scarlet artery-blood cleanses away our scarlet sins (Isa.1:18). Like the heart-beat and breathing, this action continuously goes on, exchanging our sin for His righteousness, our death for His life (Eph.2:1; John 3:16) and our weakness for His strength. The life-giving oxygen is the breath of God, the Holy Spirit, doing the work of sanctification (purifying—1 Pet.1:22) in us, as we keep on filling our spiritual lungs with His presence (Eph.5:18).

After cancer surgery, my doctor ordered me to walk in the fresh air, filling my lungs and my body cells with oxygen. He said, "Cancer can't live in the presence of oxygen." Neither can sin exist in the presence of the Holy Spirit. Either the sin in our lives will quench the Spirit (1 Thes.5:19; Eph.4:30-32), or the Spirit will replace it with righteousness (Eph.5:8-11). Relinquish the deadly carbon dioxide, and receive His oxygen! Choose LIFE!

73
VERTIGO

$\mathcal{A}$fter cancer surgery, my traumatized colon was taking a long time to settle down, causing me a lot of digestive distress. A friend recommended a kinesiologist who could get my body back into balance. I was desperate, so I started treatments. The use of magnets, crystals and 'body-talk' seemed weird, like some sort of New Age thing, but I kept hoping it would help. Several months into the 'therapy', I asked the practitioner about doing calisthenics, so she gave me a few sheets of paper explaining some floor exercises. As I took them from her, I noticed on the introductory page that these exercises had been developed in a Buddhist monastery. I said I wasn't comfortable with that, but she told me to ignore it, and just do the movements.

It was a while before I purchased a mat, and began my 'fitness regime'; but about a week into it, halfway through the moves one morning, the ceiling, walls and floor of my room started to swirl in on me, as dizziness and nausea gripped me. After a few minutes, it gradually subsided. That evening, as I lay down in bed, it returned, worse this time. I began to panic, thinking I might be having a heart attack. I called for an ambulance, but the hospital examination revealed no physical reason for the vertigo!

I tried exercising again, but the dizziness returned with certain movements, so I stopped. However, every night, with the motion of lying down, and also of sitting up in bed in the morning, the dizziness would hit me, just for a few seconds. This continued for six weeks, until I woke up one morning to the voice of God asking me, "Eunice, what were you doing when the dizziness started?" As soon as I said "exercises", I knew that I had bowed down to the god Buddha, or the Yoga spirit, as my head was bent back in the Cobra position. I gasped "That's idolatry!" My next words were of repentance and renunciation, as I recognized this spirit of idolatry that I had opened the door to. Then, in the name of Jesus, and the authority of the Holy Spirit, I cast out that spirit. Immediately, a snake-like movement flowed through and out of my body, from the neck down, and the relief was instantaneous. I began to praise God—for the deliverance, and for showing me that what was in me was from the evil one. Satan wanted me to suffer, but God wanted me well (Psa.103:3; Matt.9:35).

There has never been any doubt in my mind since, that Satan is real, and we play into his hands when we participate in anything even remotely connected to New Age or Eastern religions. I also have no doubt that God has given us authority over the demons and evil spirits, because Jesus defeated them at the cross (Luke 9:1; Col.2:15; Heb.2:14). By the way, the dizziness was gone from that day on, until . . . but that's another chapter!

74

A DRY AND THIRSTY LAND

It was a period of a year that I had spent returning on a regular basis to the kinesiologist, with each succeeding appointment date being determined by *what my body told her as she laid her hand on my arm!* It was towards the end of that year that my friend gave me the book I mentioned in chapter 15. It was because of the teaching by Henry Wright that I was given the insight into the reason for the dizziness I was experiencing, and as a result I was delivered from it. As I read "A More Excellent Way", I became convinced that I needed to quit the kinesiology sessions, repenting of having been *deceived* into thinking it was a God-blessed form of healing, and of participating in it.

Along with that, I knew within me that not only had I obtained **no** relief from my digestive problems, there were several things that the enemy stole from me during that year. That's what he does, you know, along with killing and destroying (John 10:10). I had spent hundreds of dollars, which I couldn't even claim on my income tax, because it was classified as alternative medicine! But, worse still, it was one of the most spiritually dry periods of my life. I still went to church, but stopped reading the Bible, praying or going to Bible studies. My joy and peace were stolen!

But praise God for His mercy, seeking me when I was not seeking Him. And praise Him for His grace in revealing His truth to me, exposing the devil's lies. I can see His hand so evident, in bringing that book to me when I was so desperate, through a friend who obeyed Him. (He told her to come to church and bring it to me!) I thank God for showing me the way back into fellowship with Him and for revealing to me His Father-love that covers all my sin and casts out all my fear. And words fail to explain the joy and peace of His abiding presence, Christ living in me by His Spirit, who leads, teaches and empowers. He has replaced Satan's bondage with His abundant life of freedom and sonship! (Rom.8:2, 15)

Satan has deceived many in the church into believing that God doesn't heal today; so we open the door to demons by seeking answers from the world (or from the underworld?) And then we wonder why the church is powerless, why we are sick in body and mind, joyless, troubled, anxious, fearful and depressed. Maybe it is because we are trusting in all sorts of healing methods based on New Age or Eastern religions, so that the God who made us, and wants to heal us, cannot. Is it not time to cast out the idols, and turn back to the life-giving God who waits to bless us with wholeness? "To you who fear My name, the Sun of Righteousness shall arise with healing in His wings." (Mal.4:2). "I pray that you may prosper and be in health" (3 John 2).

75
WITCHCRAFT

*S*oon after the events of the previous chapter, Pastor Henry Wright came to Calgary for a conference on spiritual roots of disease. Since I had read his book, and been greatly impacted by its truth, I was delighted to hear more. One of the topics he addressed was the pathway of thought from the spirit-world into our human spirit through theta brain-waves. This pathway is used by the Holy Spirit to renew our minds by the Word of God; but evil spirits can use the same pathway to train us in the law of sin. This accounts for the battle that goes on in our mind (Rom.7:14-24). (Theta brain waves are from four to seven beats per second, the drumbeat used by witchdoctors to allow access of evil spirits into the minds of those under their power.)

A short time later, and about six weeks after my last bout of vertigo, I woke up at 3:00 a.m. with a thumping in my head, nausea and crazy dizziness. As I was crawling back to bed after dealing with the nausea, I was asking God "Why is this back? Why is the enemy messing with me?" I immediately remembered the pounding in my head, and thought 'drumbeats'. AHA!! Seven years earlier I had spent a couple of weeks in Ghana, during which time I heard the far-off beat of the shaman drums at night.

I was so relieved—not that this had been a pathway for the enemy into my mind, but that I was now onto his tricks, and he didn't stand a chance. He had overstepped his bounds, sneaking in the back door with the spirit of witchcraft, knowing that at the time I was ignorant of his schemes (2 Cor.2:11). I immediately cast out this spirit, repenting of entertaining it, and thanking God for unveiling this 'ghost from the past', so I could be rid of it by the authority of That Name at which the demons flee! I have not had even a hint of dizziness/vertigo since that time! Praise God!

I have heard believers from Africa testify that they have been so aware of the *evil* spirit-world, that when they "turn to God from idols" (1 Thes.1:9), they understand and embrace the work, power and communication of the *Holy* Spirit in their lives. The fear-instilling spirits have been replaced with the Spirit of peace, comfort and love. It is ironic, and very sad that many of us in the western world are afraid of this amazing gift of the Spirit of Christ in us. We are content to live on an earthly plane, quenching and grieving the Holy Spirit, thus annulling His power in us, unaware of His presence or His gifts. Thus we fall prey to the voices of the very evil one that Jesus came to destroy. We accept *his* lies while rejecting the Truth. Why, after being supernaturally born again by the Spirit, do we ignore Him and deny the Supernatural for the rest of our lives? What a travesty of God's grace!! (Heb.10:29; Gal.3:3) Whose voice are we listening to? (Rom.7:14-24; 12:1-2)

76
I'M SCARED!

*M*any years ago, when I travelled by train through the Rocky mountains to the west coast of Canada, I was glad it was a night trip, so I wouldn't have to see where I was – perched on the edges of cliffs, with huge, deep canyons below. (I would shut my eyes if I was in a car on hilly roads with no guard rails.) Yes, I had a fear of heights, and never liked to live higher up in a building than the second floor, or go near the edge of anything tall.

But, in the summer of 2010, I drove a friend from Calgary to a Youth Camp near Princeton, B.C., along the twisting narrow roads of the old highway, and over the high, modern, fast-paced Coquihalla, with almost a reckless abandon, facing the heights and chasms fearlessly. What made the difference? The answer is both simple and profound. Let me share it with you.

As a proviso, we need to distinguish between 1) a <u>healthy, built-in fear</u> that allows us to sense danger and react appropriately; 2) a <u>reverential fear of God</u> that leads to awe, worship and a desire for holiness; and 3) <u>fear connected to stress and anxiety,</u> that binds and paralyzes, often becomes phobic, and is programmed into us by real or imaginary events in our lives that Satan uses to reinforce a spirit of fear in us. This latter fear is the problem.

I learned several things about this <u>crippling fear</u>:

1) It is <u>a spirit</u>, and is <u>not from God</u>. "God has not given us a spirit of fear, but of power and of love and of a sound mind" (2 Tim.1:7). See Rom.8:15. Fear is <u>from Satan</u> (Gen.3:9-11.)

2) Fear is <u>a sin</u>, and is <u>the antithesis of faith</u> (Rom.14:23; John 14:1; Luke 8:50). If I am in fear I am not trusting God.

3) As sin, fear needs <u>to be repented of</u>; and as an evil spirit, it needs <u>to be cast out</u> in Jesus' name (Luke 24:47; 11:20).

4) As we embrace and walk in the perfect love of God, we will have no fear. <u>Perfect love casts out fear</u> (1 John 4:16, 18).

When I recognized my fears as sin, repented of them, renounced their power in my life, and cast them out in the name of Jesus; and when I began to trust God's perfect love implicitly for every need, and in every circumstance, the fears began to dissipate, replaced by the peace He promised (John 14:27; Phil.4:6-7)

In 1968, I lost my bearings in the middle of Nairobi, Kenya, and was gripped with fear when a man started to follow me. Finally, in desperation, I swung around and shouted out the words "Get lost!" He slunk away, and faded into the crowd. . . In 2010 I got lost in Calgary, and was whistling and singing the words of Psa.34:1-4, but couldn't remember the last verse. Finally, I found my way, and as I walked through the door of my home, the words came to me: "I sought the LORD, and He heard me, and delivered me from all my fears." Indeed, He has!!

77
FALLING OR FLYING?

*P*robably fifteen years ago my church was having a week-end retreat at a Bible campground. My friend, who was almost my age, wanted to ride the zip-line; and not to be outdone, I decided I would as well. It was designed for children, so was quite a short ride propelled by gravity along a cable from a high platform to a lower one. I watched my friend go down, then I was fastened into the safety harness, which was then clipped on to the cable. I was sitting on the edge of the platform, when I was told I had to push myself off – as in, <u>jump</u>. Suddenly I was not so sure about this, and I begged to be pushed. That apparently wasn't an option, so I finally fought my fear, and forced myself to take the plunge. The slide began, and my screams echoed my fear. Then my harness flipped around, propelling me blindly towards the lower platform. At the last second I turned and saw a friendly hand reached out to avert a crash. Whew!!

Three years ago, at seventy-three, I rode a much higher and longer zip-line at a youth camp. We climbed hundreds of steps to the platform, and I chose to do the Superman ride, flying like a bird over the beautiful lake and mountain slopes near Princeton, B.C. This time I was excited, but not afraid. I waited for the jump-off cue, but my feet were suddenly gently lifted upward, as the harness, fastened at my waist at the back, swung me into prone position, and I was in controlled flight. It was amazing, as at first I flapped my arms with joy, then just soared, with total peace and lack of fear, drinking in the scenery below. Too soon it was over, and my feet were back on terra firma.

We can go through the experiences of life with either fear or faith, slipping or soaring, falling or flying, screaming or singing. As we learn to trust our loving heavenly Father, our fears will vanish in His love. Life will be an adventure faced with anticipation, not a dark and dangerous journey filled with anxiety. As a child I sang a little song that reminds me of this truth, and of Matt.6:25-34:

"Said the robin to the sparrow, 'I should really like to know Why these anxious human beings rush about and worry so.' Said the sparrow to the robin, 'Friend, I think that it must be That they have no heavenly Father, such as cares for you and me!'" (Tune–'What a Friend we have in Jesus')

I may never bungee jump, parachute from an airplane or down-hill ski. But I know that wherever God puts me, I am safe, and do not need to be afraid. Many fearful things may face us in the future, but we are safe in His pavilion, and under His wings. The words of Psa.91 still stand, unrevoked and eternally dependable!

78
THE PSYCH WARD

One of the most distressing and depressing moments I have ever experienced was when I recently walked through the halls of the Psychiatric ward at a local hospital. The walls were lined with the art work of the patients – paintings done by people whose minds have been blighted by the great destroyer and deceiver himself, "that serpent of old, called the devil and Satan" (Rev.12:9). These pictures were dark, eerie, harsh, strident, evil – a display in stark and horrific image, of the dastardly work of destruction by the enemy, in the minds of his victims imprisoned behind the closed doors. They are marginalized, forgotten, mistreated, and stupefied with drugs so the evil within them can't manifest. Each and every one of them is a declaration by Satan that says: "God's masterpiece? HAH!! **Look at them! They're mine, now!"**

What ever happened to so defile and twist and distort the fabric of their life, that they are left here to die like caged animals? Was it repeated sexual abuse by one who was supposed to love and protect them? Is this what made them create another personality in their mind to hide behind in their shame? Is that what destroyed their sense of worth, and led them into a life of drugs and self-destruction? Was it because they have never experienced love and nurturing; only rejection, neglect and verbal abuse? Was it because of deep betrayal by a parent, a spouse, or friend? Whatever it was, we know this was not what God desired for these people made in His image. This, as was already pointed out, is the trademark work of the enemy of our souls who comes to steal, kill and destroy (John 10:10).

Would it have made a difference if these dear tormented souls had realized that the God who made them, loved them and wanted the very best for them? What if someone along their pathway had shown them love and cared about them out of a pure heart? It has been seen recently that some people with schizophrenia have improved remarkably when just one person took a personal interest in, and loved them as they were. Spending time with them was key to their healing.

May God give us compassion for those who are hurting, and take us out of our self-centered aloofness, to reach out with a smile, a helping hand, and intercessory prayer to those around us who need to know that someone cares. Jesus operated out of love and compassion in all his contacts with those who were hurt and cast-out (Matt.9:35-36; John 8:10-11; Heb.4:15). As His followers, we are to do the same (Heb.13:3; Rom. 12:15; Matt.18:33; 1 Pet.3:8; Gal.6:1-2; 1 John 3:16-18, 4:20-21; 1 Cor.13). Let us, in love, give that "cup of cold water" in Jesus' name! (Mark 9:41)

79
TELLING A STORY

*M*ost people learn more from pictures than from words, possibly because from the time we are born, and have eyes to see, we are surrounded by real, live, moving creatures, as well as non-living objects and scenes that may or may not be moving. Long before we can adequately express our needs or feelings, we have been learning by observing our surroundings. We broaden our scope of learning through pictures of things outside our environment. Reading, of course, comes later, and words written with pen and ink on paper, paint pictures in our minds, of things and places we may not ever see with our physical eyes.

When an artist takes his brush to the canvas, he is telling a story. So, too, the colors and strokes that are painted on the fabric of our lives by our heritage, environment, and ultimately God, tell our story. We have absorbed colors of every hue into the fibers of our being. But often, the soft, fresh tones of innocence are lost beneath strident pigments of harsh reality—dark hurts of the soul and spirit, coming from people who *should have* loved us, nourished our souls, and at all costs protected our innocence. Instead they have betrayed our trust, and defiled us. So we hide our life-canvas in shame, or cover it with a false bravado.

I will be eternally grateful for parents who protected the canvas of my life from harm, so I did not have to bear an undeserved shame or guilt like a pall over my life. I cannot imagine the pain of such a secretive burden. So when God began to lead me into a ministry that involves discerning the roots of physical, emotional and mental diseases, and walking through a process of healing and deliverance, my heart ached with love and compassion for so many hurting people. It has been a wakeup call to the evil of men who live with generational spirits of lust, perversion, cruelty, alcoholism, control and abuse. They perpetuate this evil against their innocent children, and they in turn, against theirs.

What is the answer? For the perpetrator, it is not rehabilitation, or jail-time or even psychotherapy. Only the Holy Spirit, by the power of the blood and the resurrection of Christ, can transform any life. At the same time, the evil spirits that have bound the family for generations must be cast out, and the right for them to wreak havoc in more lives cancelled through repentance and restoration. Those abused must *separate the sinner from the sin*, realizing that it was evil spirits in the person that made them do what they did. *This enables them to forgive*, be healed and restored, freed from the pain, guilt and shame, by receiving God's love and forgiveness. The canvas is wiped clean, and new, vibrant colors applied by God's hand will bring glory to Him (Isa.61:1-3; 1 Cor.6:9-11).

80
THE FAMILY TREE

$\mathscr{A}$t our family reunion a few years ago, we were treated to a power-point presentation amazingly crafted by my niece. She has spent countless hours researching and digging to put together our family tree, tracing our gene-alogy back several generations. I had never been interested in the history of my ancestors—in fact I didn't like any sort of history. But this wasn't just boring dates and events. It was personal stories of the lives of real people—*my people*! I found out that as a young man, my grandfather, William, farmed in North Dakota, USA. A few miles away, in Canada, lived a young couple with one child. The husband died sud-denly, and Will began helping the widow, Sarah, take care of her farm. Eventually he married her, moving to Canada, where they homesteaded. I never knew them, nor her son, Uncle George, who died in the First World War; but I spent my first seven years in their large two-story stone house, playing in the barn-loft and spacious yard, and roaming through the fields.

(Many people are afraid their generational tree will reveal family secrets—that skeleton in the closet: a criminal, a crook or a child born out of wedlock; alcoholism or insanity; an abu-sive spouse or mother; a child predator or a profligate son, a rapist or a harlot).

When we make our first visit to a doctor, we normally have to complete a questionnaire on our medical history, such as what diseases our parents or grandparents had. This is because many diseases are hereditary (Deut.28:58-59), due to the curse of sin. Disease isn't the only thing that can attach itself to our DNA. A spirit of occultism, lust, rage, perversion, fear, jealousy etc. that has manifested in a parent, often shows up in the child, maybe at unpredictable times, and even though they have never been in contact with the parent. In the Bible, the word iniquity is often used for these generational sins (Neh.9:2; Ezra 9:6-7; Psa.51:5).

When we are faced with an inherited disease, often a connection can be made with a generational spirit. If, by the discernment of the Holy Spirit we are able to recognize this, we can repent of it both for ourselves and for our generations, and in the Name of Jesus, by the authority he has given us, we can cast out that spirit, cancelling its assignment against us and our family. This results in the healing of the disease, and protection against it and familial spirits for the future generations! (Exod.20:6-7)

It is time for us as God's representatives here on earth to learn to discern evil spirits, not to fear them, but to use our authority to cast them out, and cleanse our 'temple' of them, allowing the Holy Spirit His rightful control in our lives, for our good, and His glory! (Heb.5:14; 1 Cor.12:10; 6:19-20; Gal.5:16-17)

81
BROKEN CONNECTIONS

*L*ike our Dad, my oldest sister, Arla, was an unpublished poet. So, in her late sixties, when she began to notice tell-tale signs of encroaching Alzheimer's disease, she recorded, in blank verse, what it was like to gradually lose touch with reality. She likened it to a winter storm, a raging blizzard whose bitter cold shrinks telephone and power lines. This, followed by a warm moisture-laden wind, loads the wires with ice and frost, and they start to snap, breaking and pulling down their supporting poles. Electricity and communication are cut off, resulting in isolation, suffering, loss, and even death.

As her own personal blizzard advanced, Arla realized some of her lines of memory were snapping. Her good friends became strangers; she didn't even recognize the woman she saw in the mirror. Her friendly kitchen became an unsolvable puzzle, and she searched for clues to find the answers. She relinquished to God her cherished memories, because she couldn't unlock the drawers of her mind to recall them. In the midst of the storm, God's love and the peace of His presence became her source of joy and strength, as she committed herself and her struggles to her coming Bridegroom, praising Him for His faithfulness.

Before she went home to be with her Lord some ten years later, Arla copied a notebook of her poems, in beautiful

Primary school teacher printing, and flawless penmanship—one book for each of her eleven living siblings. It was a labor of love, and a treasure of literature to be cherished by her family. Thank you, dear sister!

Traumas in our life can often disconnect us from God, and havoc is wreaked when we are overcome by the storms that assail. How can we keep connected in such times? I quote another poem that Arla wrote, which along with "Blizzards", I read at her memorial service. It speaks of her unwavering trust in God, and her total submission to His will—an unbroken connection—one of the secrets to her godly life and the legacy of faith she left us.

"<u>MY PRAYER</u>

If Thy refining fire, fierce and purifying,
Is needed to purge from me all dross,
And if Thy molding hammer, true and relentless,
Is needed to bring forth in me Thy image,
Then let the fire and hammer purge and mold
'Til all shall see in me
Thee only,
Unclouded,
Unblurred,
Beautiful as Thou truly art.
Amen"

As purified gold, her life reflected the image of her beloved Lord!

82
WATCH YOUR STEP!

*A*rmed with plastic buckets and anticipation, my friend, her daughter and I headed down the Britannia Slopes of Calgary into River Park, which runs along the banks of the Elbow River. The time seemed right to find ripe berries on the Saskatoon bushes along the paths. Soon our buckets began to fill with these tasty morsels, as we talked and laughed, enjoying the beautiful day.

I spotted a cluster of berries on a high branch, and reached up, as I stepped forward onto the thick grassy carpet under the bushes. Big mistake! Beneath the grass was . . . nothing, and my foot was going down over an embankment, taking the rest of me with it. As the berries, jolted out of the bucket, flew up into my face, I had the presence of mind to grab onto the overhanging bushes. I was swung around, and suddenly my head, arms and feet were all pointed skyward. The branches slipped from my grasp and I found myself sliding backwards down the steep slope towards the river, still clutching the handle of my empty bucket. Suddenly with another jolt, the back of my head slammed into a tree at the water's edge, bringing me to an abrupt halt! In spite of the pain in my head I started to laugh out loud, and my friends peered through the bushes to see the ridiculous sight!

The book of Proverbs contains much of God's wisdom that He had bestowed on Solomon (1 Kings 4:29). In this book there are numerous warnings to "watch your step" i.e. Prov.4:26-27. What seems like a safe place to go, or looks inviting, may, in fact, lead to disaster and pain. If your friends are inviting you into questionable paths, "do not walk with them, keep your foot from their path" (1:15). Even if everybody else is doing it, and it feels right, stepping outside of God's plan for our relationships leads to sorrow, regret, shame and heartache (Prov.2:16-19; 6:24-29).

The secret to avoiding pitfalls is found in the first six verses of chapter three: *obey God's word, hold onto truth, trust God, not your own wisdom,* and *"in all your ways acknowledge Him, and He will direct your paths"*. With God's wisdom and discretion you "will walk safely in your way, and your foot will not stumble" v.23

At the Bible School I attended, we read through the Book of Proverbs once a month – every day at breakfast a chapter was read by one of the staff or students. Recently I have been doing this, and realizing that it's a wonderful "How-To" manual for life, and wisdom for all the issues and problems we face daily, and for those that come upon us suddenly. As you go through this "Book of Wisdom", prays for God's wisdom to fill your soul, so your steps will be directed into the paths of peace. See Prov.3:13-18.

83
TEN-POINT LANDING

was walking the few blocks from the bus stop to the doctor's office, at my usual rapid pace, when suddenly my foot stumbled and my body began hurtling through the air like an out-of-control airplane, on a downward grade towards the concrete sidewalk. I'm not sure what part of me landed first, but my hands were scraped, plus my knees. My big toes must have hit end-on, judging from the black nails that appeared shortly after. My belly and elbows hit at some point, seemingly unharmed, while my head also had a fairly gentle landing. Not so my left shoulder – the same one involved in the skate-boarding incident some ten years earlier, when my collar bone was broken! This time, it didn't seem to be broken, but was extremely painful.

When I dragged my sorry-looking self into the doctor's office a few minutes later, I received immediate attention to my bleeding hand, and orders to go for X-rays on my shoulder. So, back to the bus for the trip downtown to a clinic near my home. They almost turned me away because I didn't have my Health Care card with me, but finally relented. More pain ensued, as the technologist unsympathetically twisted my arm into numerous contortionist positions. I shuffled home, body aching, and shoulder screaming.

At home, I found the sling from my prior accident, and soon my shoulder was thanking me for the relief it felt. I phoned the next day and heard what I already knew – nothing was broken. With information from the internet, and by talking to therapist friends and others, I concluded that I had a rotator cuff tear. I soon tired of the sling, and just kept using my arm. Within ten days I was able to raise it over my head and swing it in wide circles in every direction. I thank God for quick, complete healing (Exod.15:26).

This incident became a time of conviction for me, because I was reminded of the scripture: "Pride goes before destruction, and a haughty spirit before a fall." (Prov.16:18) I didn't think I was proud about anything. But God knows us so much better than we do, and He showed me that there was spiritual pride in my heart. According to Jonathan Edwards, this is right from the pit of Hell, and a prime weapon of Satan to bring error, and hinder the work of God. Instead of realizing like Paul, that "I have nothing that I did not receive", and there is no room for boasting (1 Cor.4:6-7; Gal.6:14), I was portraying the attitude that I had the truth; I had arrived, as opposed to so many who hadn't. So a sort of spiritual superiority permeated my thinking, speaking and writing. I have recognized this, and am so sorry about any whom I have offended. I repented and received God's forgiveness. May I do everything in the spirit of humility, as I banish pride from my life in the name of Jesus! (2 Tim.2:24-25; Tit.3:2; 1 Pet.5:5)

84
GETTING OFF TRACK

I was approaching the intersection, prepared to make a right turn onto a main thoroughfare, when lights and signs warned "<u>CONSTRUCTION – EXPECT DELAYS</u>". Pylons were placed to redirect traffic. As I peered ahead into the darkness, I saw a sign showing No Right Turn from the lane I was in. Just then I saw a gap in the row of pylons, and concluded that I needed to move into the curb lane. Soon I ran out of pavement, at the edge of a sharp drop onto the street which had been dug out for repaving.

In my rear-view mirror I could see that the car behind had followed me, so motioned to him to back up, so that I in turn could back up. But he was blocked by a third car behind him! So, making another foolish decision, I eased the car over the ledge, realizing too late how big a drop it was (probably four inches).

The next few minutes I provided some free entertainment for the people waiting at the light, and for the construction workers whose trucks were parked several rods ahead. I turned this way and that, looking for a way out. Finding none, I drove towards the trucks and stopped, my headlights glaring into the blackness. Soon a truck came towards me, and the driver approached my car. I asked, "Is there a way out of here?" His answer was a question, "How did you get *in* here?" So I told him about the gap in the 'fence', and he hurried off to fix it, and to steer the other 'sheep' back onto the right road. When he returned he said I had to back out where I came in, slowly, and at an angle. I hurriedly pleaded, "Could you drive?" I watched as he maneuvered first one back tire, then the other, followed by the first front tire, then the other, over that painful step up and out of the trap. This kind man then acted as traffic cop, holding back cars until I was safely on the right track. As I approached the corner, I realized that the sign said "No Turn <u>on Red</u>". I had read only half the message!

Summing up, and applying a spiritual lesson:

- I trespassed, and led others astray. (Isa.53:6a)
- My error got me into a bad situation. (Prov.14:12)
- I tried to no avail to extricate myself. (Tit.3:5)
- Someone was there to rescue me, and he did it gladly, without reprimanding or scolding me. (John 3:17)
- All I had to do was ask, relinquish control, and put him in the driver's seat. (Rom.10:13; 6:13)
- This same kind rescuer put me on the right road, and blessed me with his words of forgiveness. (Psa.40:2-3)

It was a well-learned lesson on the grace of God in our lives!

85
BRUISES

$\mathcal{I}$ like to buy plain yogurt, and add my own fruit, preferably a tropical fruit like mango or pineapple. I was looking forward to a kiwi-yogurt treat last month, and selected one of the ripe kiwis from my fridge. As I began to prepare it I noticed a tiny little break in the skin, and found a deep, nasty discoloring beneath it. In fact it was starting to spoil and rot. Not wanting to throw it out, I cut around the wound and the decay, confiscating what I could. I wondered what had happened to my little fuzzy friend. Had someone dropped it? Did someone's dirty thumbnail break through its skin? Did a hungry insect or small animal try to take a bite out of it? Whatever the case, it was damaged, bruised, traumatized, and had become less than what it was made to be.

When a part of our body receives a hard blow, the tiny blood vessels just beneath the skin break, and the blood spills out into the tissues, and begins to decay, darkening the skin with an ugly bruise. As these blood cells break down they are gradually flushed away by the body's natural processes, and the bruise goes away. God designed our body so it would heal itself, fight disease, and resist infection. Hmm! I wonder if He *added* these defenses, *after* the curse of disease was brought on by man's sin!

We may have gone through traumas that can wound and bruise the soul and spirit as well as the body. Abuse of all kinds, death of loved ones, a horrible experience or witnessing a terrible accident are examples of this. Sometimes traumas happen at conception, birth, or early childhood, and are compounded by continuing trauma throughout life. Do the deep hurts of these traumas heal with time? Or do they stay in us and cause disruptions in our mental and physical health? Perhaps we have buried them in the deep, dark recesses of our being, and forgotten them. But they grow and fester, and the putrefaction eventually spills out in anger, bitterness, depression and disease, which we can't understand, explain or control.

When Jesus says "Come to me, all you who are weighed down and weary, and I will give you rest", He is speaking to people who have been traumatized. He spoke these words in fulfillment of Isaiah's prophecy "By His stripes we are healed". The blood that flowed from His veins as He was flogged is sufficient to heal every wound of our soul and spirit. This includes our emotions, our minds, our feelings, and our pain. He will give you joy for mourning, praise to replace your heaviness, and healing for your broken heart (Isa.53:4-5, 61:1-3). Go to Him – give Him the hurt you are carrying, and let His love and grace heal you to the core of your being. It's what He wants for you. It's what you need!

86
"LITTLE MISS PIGGY"

$\mathcal{I}$ have been blessed (or cursed) with a good appetite, and a stomach with a huge capacity and extraordinary elasticity. At a church picnic recently someone asked me what I like, and all I could come up with was 'food' and 'eating'! So on the name tag she made for me, she drew a picture of a chef's hat, a tray of food, and a smiley 'me'. The next morning I woke up with a stomach hangover, literally. It wasn't aching in the normal sense of the word – it was just really sore, for several hours. Now here I am again with a very hurting midriff, the morning after another barbecue pot luck meal within five days. This time, the word 'gluttony', and the warning in Prov.23:1-2 are floating through my mind. I recognize my 'sin', and I repent, even as I write this.

At first I rationalized that I don't 'pig-out' all the time. At home I restrict my meal-sizes to a normal portion. But when I see all that wonderful, tantalizing food made by other people, I just can't seem to stop until I'm groaningly full, or all the food is gone, whichever comes first. Have you ever watched a pig eat? It's not a pretty sight. There's nothing sedate or polite about it. In fact, it's disgusting! As Phil.3:19 says, "their god is their belly". Ouch! That hit home with me. Thank You, Holy Spirit for convicting me!

By now, you may be thinking I am taking this whole over-eating thing much too seriously. The fact is, I could be talking about any number of bad habits, that are like weights around our ankles, or snares that entangle us in the race of our life in Christ. Heb.12:1 reminds us that in order to run the race, and finish it with joy, we need to lay aside these sins that impede our progress (Col.3:8-10; Eph.4:22-32). If we decide to change, and begin striving, we lose heart and thus lose the battle. But by calling these habits sin, repenting of them and receiving forgiveness, we recognize that just as we could do nothing to save ourselves from sin, only God's grace can deliver us from our sinful habits (1 John 1:8-10).

It comes down, really, to idolatry. Anything in our life that is not to the glory of God; that we cater to in order to satisfy our cravings; that we do to excess; or that is harmful to our minds or bodies, is an idol that steals our hearts from God (1 John 2:16, 5:21; Jas.1:13-16, 4:1; Eph.5:18). In truth, He is the only One who can satisfy the longings in our soul (Psa.107:9, 34:8). No amount of shopping, partying, face-booking, video-gaming, web-surfing, texting, alcohol, drugs or eating, etc. can fill the aching void in our heart that only God can fill with His love (John 6:35; 7:37-39).

"Trust...in the living God, who gives us richly all things to enjoy" (1 Tim.6:17). "Know the love of Christ which passes knowledge, that you may be filled with all the fullness of God (Eph.3:19).

87
ADDICTED!

*O*n five days of the week, I can walk a couple of blocks to pick up two free newspapers, and quite often I do – not to keep up with the latest sensational news, but for the Crossword Puzzles. I try to rationalize this habit, since the price is right, it keeps my mind sharp (?), and it is harmless. Recently, when I went onto the internet to find the answer to a clue, I found a lot of websites that offered free crossword puzzles, some of which I could do online. They even told me when I made a mistake, kept track of how long I took to finish, and sounded bells and whistles of congratulation when the last letter was added. It was actually quite exciting . . . and addicting!

I did one, then another, and another, each time trying to beat my best time. I lost track of the hour, and the number of puzzles I did, until my eyes were sore and bloodshot, and I was bone-tired and hungry. I pictured myself in front of a slot machine, waiting for the big win (and I didn't like the picture!) I asked myself why I needed to compete with myself, why I would waste hours on this exercise, and what I should do. It really was looking a lot like an addiction, one definition of which is 'trying to fill a void caused by a lack of, or need for, love'. This didn't fit with what I had learned about God's all-encompassing love for me, His child. Wasn't His affirmation of me enough? What more could self-effort offer?

Instead of drinking from God's pure living water, I was seeking satisfaction at broken cisterns (Jer.2:13). I recognized my need to repent and return to the only One who can satisfy.

Out of curiosity I checked, and found one reference to addiction in the Bible, in 1 Cor.16:15 (KJV), where Paul writes that the household of Stephanas "have addicted themselves to the ministry of the saints". That sounds like a pretty good addiction to have. It is noteworthy that in newer translations this word *addicted* is translated 'devoted'. You see, anything we become addicted to becomes an object of devotion. We may devote our time, energy or money to this thing, with the result that it replaces God in our thinking and in our worship. Good things can take the place of the Best. We may not bow down in worship to an idol, but if we are looking to something or someone other than God to fulfill our needs, or if that thing or person is our main focus of attention, it indeed has become an idol! The idols in our heart are just as real and dangerous as idols on the shelf. So, in response to John's admonition in I John 5:21, to "keep yourselves from idols", let us ask God to show us the idols in our life, and let us rid our heart and our home of idols of any kind. Let us give all our worship to God, who alone is worthy of our devotion. "No man can serve two masters" (Matt.6:24).

88

ONE THING LEADS TO ANOTHER

mentioned in the previous chapter that I was surfing the net for crossword puzzles. Well, in my search I was drawn in by yet another idol, named Sudoku. I could spend hours trying to fit the numbers into that little grid, sometimes having to start over two or three times before solving the puzzle. What *is* a puzzle, and why do I find it so tantalizing? I learned that a puzzle is a game or contrivance designed to test one's skill, intelligence, ingenuity or patient effort. Hmmm. I have to ask myself "Am I so insecure that I need a puzzle to give me a sense of worth, or to validate my innate abilities?" It's like using alcohol to bolster confidence. It goes without saying that I had to over-indulge on Sudokus before being able to admit I had a second addiction.

I realized that not only was this another idol in my life, but it was feeding my pride. After all, not everyone has the intelligence to be able to do a Sudoku, or the perseverance to conquer really difficult ones! As I thought about this, it came to me that next to idol-worship, pride is probably what God hates most. (It tops His 'hate-list' in Prov.6:16-19!) Lucifer's pride led to his banishment from heaven. The book of Proverbs has a lot to say about pride, none of it good (Prov.8:13; 11:2; 13:10; 14:3; 16:18; 29:23).

If we really think about it, pride is a form of idol-worship, where I, myself, become my own idol. Instead of realizing that every- thing we are and have is a gift from God, and humbly thanking Him for it, we boast in our skills and accomplishments as if it was all our doing. Rom.1:21-23 shows where this leads—to idolatry!

Pride has many facets. It can manifest as scorn, a condescending, haughty or disdainful look, prejudice, put-downs, egoism, self-centeredness, pretentiousness, bullying, and the like. None of these is fitting for a child of God. Our mandate is expressed in Phil.2:3-8—"Let nothing be done through selfish ambition or conceit, but in lowliness of mind let each esteem others better than himself. . . Let this mind be in you which was also in Christ Jesus. . . Who humbled Himself, and became obedient to death." We see here that the opposite of pride is humility. See Jas.4:6, 10 and 1 Pet.5:5-6. Also look at Psa.18:27; Prov.15:33; 22:4. Notice that God rewards humility with riches, honor and life!

I believe it takes humility to admit you have pride, and to repent of it; and when we have humility there is no more room for pride. They are mutually exclusive. Remember, it was Satan who lifted himself up in pride; and it was Jesus who abased Himself in humility, in order to die on the cross for us, setting us free from the "lust of the flesh, the lust of the eyes and the pride of life" (1 John 2:16). Look at God's promise to the humble in Isa.57:15!

89

"THE RAINS CAME DOWN"

"*A*nd the floods came up". Few who lived in Alberta during June, 2013 will ever forget the destruction and devastation that struck all across the province when rivers overflowed their banks, and huge walls of water slammed into houses, bridges and roads, upheaving lives and crushing hopes. Prime riverside property, eroded away, became unsafe and unsightly. Thousands of people became homeless, or at least were evacuated for days or weeks, waiting to see if their home could be restored. Business places were ravished, along with millions of dollars' worth of inventory.

As the waters began to abate, thousands of eager volunteers from all over descended on the flood scene, with boots, gloves, shovels, pumps, trucks, bulldozers—anything that could be used to clear out the water, mud and debris. Others provided food and water for the evacuees and volunteers. Children raised funds by selling lemonade or cookies. The Police, Fire Department and Army worked long and hard to ensure safety on all fronts. The Utility companies mustered all their resources to restore power, gas and safe water supplies. Donations of funds were made to the different disaster relief agencies. Empty buildings were used as temporary shelters. The Government provided pre-loaded cash cards to evacuees, and promises of continued support.

We had watched it rain, day after dreary day. At the same time, the winter snows were melting in the mountains, further swelling the rising rivers. But we were so unprepared for the floods when they came. Similarly, decade after decade, people watched as Noah prepared lumber, then methodically and precisely built a huge ark to house his family and a whole zoo load of animals. Did they heed the signs of coming disaster? It seems that life went on as usual and they did not realize what was coming until it was upon them (Matt.24:38-39). Notice the word of warning in vs.42 and 44, to watch and be ready, because <u>Jesus is coming when we do not expect Him, to take His own to be with Him (John 14:3).</u>

The life-style of Noah's day is described in Gen.6 as 'wicked', "evil", "corrupt and filled with violence". Sound familiar? Is our generation becoming like the people in Noah's day? God used a world-wide flood to cleanse the earth of corruption— destroying several generations of degraded people, among whom Noah shone as a just and perfect man who walked with God. Noah and his immediate family were the only people saved from the flood. <u>Let us be diligent to walk with God, abiding in Him, separated from the evil of the world, confident of Whose we are and Whom we serve, so we are not either embarrassed or ashamed to stand before Him when Christ returns</u> (1 John 2:28).

90
BREAKING SOUL-TIES

People have occasionally told me they couldn't figure me out, and my usual answer was, "Well, if you ever do, let me know." I didn't understand why I had this sort of 'straddle the fence' way of living, which manifested quite early on. Why couldn't I be like my older sister, ridiculously good and obedient, who never got into trouble? Was it peer pressure, wanting to fit in, even where I knew I didn't belong? It was gratifying to be accepted, and there was a sense of excitement in 'treading on thin ice'; but I also tried not to overstep the line of my strict moral upbringing. There was a constant struggle between my desires and my conscience, and I am glad that for the most part, my conscience would rein me in. I really admired my sister's steadfast example of integrity, and it helped to keep me focused on my calling to follow Jesus.

At different times throughout my life, I have had relationships that were a very negative influence on me, as I daresay is true with most people. 1 Cor.15:33 warns us: "Do not be deceived: Evil company corrupts good habits". The book of Proverbs is rife with examples of this, and Solomon, as one who had many harmful alliances, repeatedly warns against the danger of them. Unhealthy relationships that pollute our soul, often knit us together with people by evil cords, in ungodly soul-ties (often called spirit-ties).

This happens wherever occultism, such as Ouija boards, fortune-telling or New Age is practiced. If a person, or their ancestors have been involved in Free Masonry, or any such lodge where rituals and oaths are a part of their membership, devastating soul-ties are formed. The same is true when sexual activity of any sort happens outside the bond of marriage, whether consensual or otherwise. Even prolonged, obsessive grief is not of God, as an ungodly tie with the deceased overtakes our lives.

Any and all of these ungodly soul-ties will keep us from living in victory; and they don't automatically disappear when we become a Christian. They can cause us to be double-minded, confused, full of dread, depressed, mentally unstable, and unable to relate to others in a healthy way, etc. In 2 Cor.6:14-18 Paul addresses this issue as it surfaced in the early church. In 2 Cor.7:1, he continues, "Let us <u>cleanse ourselves from all filthiness of the flesh and spirit</u>." In godly sorrow, let us *repent* of these ungodly soul-ties in our lives, as per verse 10. Then, in Jesus' name, and by the authority of the Holy Spirit, we need to *break them off* our self, and out of our life. When we do, they have no more power in us or over us. *Invite the Holy Spirit to renew your mind with the truth*, in place of that fear-based, lie-riddled, ungodly pattern of thinking that is from the enemy. "God has not given us a spirit of fear, but of power, and of love, and of <u>a sound mind</u>." (2 Tim.1:7)

91
DON'T TOUCH!

In a few weeks, a couple of my friends will be arriving in Israel for a ten-day tour under the leadership of renowned Bible teacher, Charles Price. This has brought back memories of my visit to the 'Holy Land' several decades ago. I had been in Ethiopia for five years, and a good friend and I were due for furlough (they call it 'home assignment' now). We decided to travel together, via Kenya, Israel and Switzerland. It was July, 1968, just thirteen months after the amazing six-day war between Israel and three of her hostile neighbors. For those who don't remember, and for others who weren't around then, the odds were definitely not on the side of the Israeli army, but God definitely was. It was like the stories of Gideon, David or Jehoshaphat from the pages of the Old Testament, when Jehovah fought for His people.

In 1967, not only were the enemy armies soundly trounced, but much of the 'Promised Land' was captured back by Israel. They took the Gaza Strip and Sinai Peninsula from Egypt; the West Bank, including East Jerusalem, from Jordan; as well as the Golan Heights from Syria. These nations found out the hard way that the nation that touches Israel touches the apple of God's eye! (Zech.2:8-9) One year later, there remained very little evidence that there had been a war!

Israel is increasingly in the news as I write, with the surrounding nations breathing out threats of annihilation. Little do they know how futile their plans are, and that all the weapons they bring against Israel will return upon them to their own destruction. They haven't learned from previous attempts, and they obviously don't know the 'rest of the story'!

Those of us who are non-Jews (Gentiles) are so indebted to the Jews, through whom we received most of the Bible, and through whom Jesus came. Jesus has made believing Jew and Gentile <u>one</u>, so we inherit the blessings of Abraham and of the New Covenant (Gal.3:6-9, 13-14, 28; Eph.2:11-19). Let us go back to chapters 9-11 in the book of Romans, and share in Paul's desire and prayer for Israel, that they may be saved (10:1). It is time for us to live out the abundant life that is ours in Christ, so that by our love and Christ-likeness, we will provoke them to jealousy (10:19; 11:11). They need to recognize in us the Messiah they still look for, so they will turn to Him for salvation.

When God blessed Abraham (Gen.12:2), this blessing included all his descendents. But with this blessing came a warning to those who would not bless his descendents (the Jewish people). In v.3 He says, "I will bless those who bless you, and I will curse him who curses you." Are we praying for the salvation of Israel? Or are we standing with those who despise and marginalize them?

92
RE-GENERATION

*R*ecently I have heard and read some teaching by Dr. Francis Myles* about the reclaiming of our God-ordained genetic make-up that has been damaged and defiled by the sins of our generations. The thing that piqued my linguistic interest, was the breakdown of the word 'regeneration' (Matt.19:28 and Tit.3:5). The word 'generation' is made up of two words—*gene* and *ration*. This suggests that the genes we have as individuals are rationed out to us according to what is in the available gene pool from all our ancestors, right back to Adam. (No wonder there are so many possibilities for diversity, even in one family!). I will not try to explain Dr. Myles' teaching*, just make a few observations.

We have likely all heard about defective or mutated genes that, if present in your 'gene ration' or mine, can cause certain diseases, abnormalities or malfunctions in the body/ mind. The only person not affected by demonic gene mutations or generational curses is Jesus Christ. He is the new Adam, perfect Son of God, untainted by the sin nature of the first Adam (Rom.5:12-19). (Before Adam sinned <u>his</u> genes were perfect too—it has been Satan's design to pollute, corrupt and contaminate the whole gene pool of humanity, originally created by God, in His image. This impure bloodline is the inheritance of all humankind).

'Regeneration' is defined in Strong's Concordance as Messianic restoration or spiritual rebirth/renovation (*i.e. a new ration of genes*). This was God's plan and purpose in our salvation – a new birth, to new life (Gal.2:20); a new creation (2 Cor.5:17); and a renewed mind (Rom.12:2). In this latter verse, and also in Eph.4:22-32 and Col.3:5-10, we see that it is up to us to put off, renounce and crucify the deeds and thoughts of the old life, and yield our bodies and souls to God the Holy Spirit to work out His new life in us, and restore what the enemy has stolen from us.

Let us suppose that the renewing of our mind means more than replacing Satan's lies with God's truth. Just as we renounce the old way of life, and put on the new, Dr. Myles contends that we must "denounce our natural lineage, for the lineage of Jesus."* Is this part of the abundant life Jesus came to give us? Just as it is not in my best interest, or that of God's kingdom, to cling to the ways of the world, the flesh and the devil, so it is fitting that I discard the lineage of the old, sinful Adam, and receive by faith the pure lineage of the new Kingly priesthood (Heb.7:11, 24-27; 1 Pet.2:9). <u>That</u>, my friend, is a mind-renewal of the highest order–the order of Melchizedek, King of righteousness! It is being a "<u>partaker of the divine nature</u>"! (2 Pet.1:4) WOW and WOW!!

*"Breaking Generational Curses under the Order of Melchizedek: Rediscovering God's Remedy to Genetic & Generational Anomalies" by Dr. Francis Myles

93
DNA

*A*ccording to Wikipedia, DNA as we know it today was discovered by scientists in the 1950's, although preliminary studies dating back to 1869 and 1928 have been documented. DNA is an amazing facet of God's creative work and wisdom that has been a mystery for hundreds of centuries. Now, to fulfill the prophecy of Dan.12:4, an explosion of knowledge, a sign of the end times, is decoding DNA, and other secrets of God (Matt.13:34). DNA is short for **D**eoxyribo**N**ucleic **A**cid. (Try saying that fast, five times!) It is not my intent here to try and explain DNA (it's much too complicated for *my* brain), but I will note some key facts.

<u>DNA is hereditary material</u>, which means it can be passed from parent to offspring via the genes. Not all its components transfer, so the DNA of a child is similar to that of the parent or a sibling, but it is also different. In fact <u>DNA "uniquely identifies a person".</u> This makes it invaluable in solving crimes. But it also emphasizes the incomprehensible vastness of God's creativity. He made each one of us singular and distinct, with our very own identity; and every one of us is known and special to Him (Psa.139). God loves us all, even when we don't give Him the time of day. "God demonstrates His own love toward us, in that while we were still sinners, Christ died for us" (Rom.5:8).

<u>Encoded in a DNA molecule are the genetic instructions for life.</u> This encoding enables us to function and develop, not as carbon copies of our parents or teachers, but to fulfill the purpose God has specifically planned for each of us individually (Eph.1:4, 11; 2:10). (However, as we saw in the previous chapter, and as the medical field attests to, our heredity components are frequently flawed. This can hinder us from fulfilling our God-designed destiny). DNA has become useful in detecting defective genes or inherited disease. On the other hand a whole ethical dilemma has emerged around the practice of human genetic engineering in disease treatment. What if there was a better way?

What if God were to download into us an 'App' that literally gave us a new DNA from Him, replacing not only defective genes, and generational curses, but our complete identity? At the close of the last chapter I quoted from 2 Pet.1:4; but later, like a lightning bolt, the words struck me. This has been God's plan from the beginning, to restore to His people the pure, untainted, undefiled DNA (which was originally in the first Adam, until he sinned), and is in the second (last) Adam – Jesus, who is "the firstborn among many brethren" (Rom.8:29). As God's children, born anew into His family, it is our birthright – a DNA straight from the Father. It makes perfect sense to receive and walk in our new identity!

Our new **<u>DNA</u>** = **<u>D</u>**ivine **<u>N</u>**ature **<u>A</u>**pplication

94
"BEFORE YOU CALL...

I live close to two grocery stores, and once a month, list in hand, I go to Co-Op and record their price for each item I need. The next day, I compare this to the First-Tuesday-of-the-Month 10% off price at Safeway, and purchase accordingly. This week, while at Co-Op, I picked up a couple of things, paid cash, and stuffed the change into my tiny red zippered purse, rearranged the groceries in the bags, and hurried off to a busy day.

That evening I couldn't find my change purse (with over $50 inside). As I looked in every possible place, I was praying that God would show me where it was. The thought came to me that I should go back to Co-Op, to see if someone had found it and turned it in. I rationalized, *as I kept searching*, that if someone found it they would very likely keep it. Finally I thanked God that He knew where it was, and He would protect it. I went to bed in peace, and slept soundly.

On my way to Safeway the next morning, I stopped at Co-Op, and headed for the service desk. I began to say something to the clerk about this being a long-shot, when suddenly I spotted it on a small table behind her. In mid-sentence I excitedly cried out, "There it is—that little red thing!" She spun around, laughed, and without a word, picked it up and handed it to me. I raised my hands and thanked God! She just kept smiling.

Many centuries ago, God spoke the following words to Isaiah the prophet concerning His people: "Before they call, I will answer: and while they are still speaking I will hear" (Isa.65:24). The onus on us is to hear Him when He answers—not with a lightning bolt or a thunderous shout, but by the inner voice of His Holy Spirit planting the thought in our mind. Why don't we hear His voice?

Many of us, whether we admit it or not, are very selective as to which of Jesus' words we choose to believe. For example, take John 14. We have no problem with the first eleven verses—that Jesus is "the way, the truth and the life". We trust that Jesus is preparing a place for us in His Father's house, and He's coming to take us there. But do we really accept that as believers we can do greater works than He did, and that the Father will give us what we ask Him for in Jesus' name? (vs.12-14) Then there is Jesus' promise to give us the Helper, the Holy Spirit (vs.16-18, 26). So often we pray for help, and then don't hear the answer, because voices from the world, from our own thinking, and from the enemy drown out the Helper's answer. Silence those voices In the name of Jesus! Tune your heart to hear His voice! (Gal.6:14; Rom.6:6-11; 1 Thes.5:19; Isa.30:21) ". . . I WILL ANSWER"!

95
CHANGING THE FILTER

 s I pulled out my vacuum cleaner last Saturday, I decided to empty the canister, since I couldn't remember doing it in a very long time. (I insert here that said dust canister is about the size of a large cooking pot.) Not surprisingly, it was almost half full of fine dust, fibers etc., compacted into a deep-dish-pie-size clump that I could lift out in basically one piece, to wrap in newspaper to go into the garbage. And then, there were the filters, one of thick, sturdy cloth stretched tautly over a wire hoop, and a paper filter beneath it. Both were disgustingly filthy, and the paper one was even torn. I cleaned off the permanent filter, replaced the paper one, put things back together, and proceeded to vacuum.

Only a few moments had passed when I realized my machine was happily (and hummingly) devouring with ease the tiny circles of paper that had escaped from the hole-punch; the occasional staple; and even those pesky bell pepper seeds that tend to fly in all directions. I wasn't having to coax it by going over an object a number of times. I almost apologized to my cleaning friend that I had been wrongly thinking it was getting old and tired, and not able to do a proper job any more. I was sorry I had not cleaned it out sooner, because now it was doing what it was meant to do, and I actually enjoyed vacuuming!

Perhaps we ask ourselves sometimes if we are really being and doing what God intended for us. Is it possible that we have allowed the filth and grime of this world to fill our senses? Our eyes and ears in particular are constantly being bombarded with soul-searing sights and sounds. If we allow these things into our mind, we lose spiritual power, and are not fulfilling the purpose for which God has created us (Eph.2:10).

Whether it is a vacuum cleaner, a furnace or a car, a clean filter is essential for optimal performance. As believers in Christ, if our minds have not been renewed by the Word of God and the Holy Spirit, we can't filter out what is evil (Tit.3:5; 2 Cor.10:5). In Jesus' prayer for us in John 17 He said that though we are in the world, we are not of the world, and that His truth would keep us separated from the world (vs.15-19). Also see 1 John 2:15-17.

Let me paraphrase Rom.12:1-2: Dear friends, I implore you to respond to God's mercy, in separating yourself from this world's enticements, to a life completely yielded to Him. This is what He desires, and it makes perfect sense (*because He bought you at great price!*) Let Him make you over from the inside out, clearing out the garbage and giving your mind a new filter (i.e. *the truth taught by the Holy Spirit*). Then you will know that His will for you is that perfect life you have been searching for!

96
100 % PURE

*M*any shoppers today have become avid label-readers, whether they are purchasing food, drink or clothing. Often they are looking for confirmation that there are no additives that could make the product less than pure, or perhaps for imitations that might pass off as the real item. Thinking about this reminded me of one of the laws God gave through Moses to Israel, under the old covenant. It's very brief, and to my knowledge only appears twice (Lev.19:19c and Deut.22:11). They were not to wear any garment of mixed fabrics, such as wool and linen. Was God just being whimsical, or was there a good reason for this edict? Why did He insist on a '100% Pure' label on their clothing?

We can speculate that He was looking ahead to the day when He would clothe His people in the pure righteousness of His Son, in the same sense that the Passover lamb, a picture of Christ, had to be without blemish. What we do know is that God Himself is pure, holy, and undefiled by sin (1 John 3:3; Psa.12:6; 18:30; Isa.6:3; Hab.1:13). He also requires purity in His children. "He chose us in Him before the foundation of the world, that we should be <u>holy and without blame</u> before Him in love" (Eph.1:4). "But as He who called you is holy, you also be <u>holy in all your conduct</u>" (1Pet.1:15-16). So what does it mean to be pure?

Though the words *pure* and *holy* come from the same Greek root, purity carries the sense of being of only one essence, with nothing added, no impurity. In Jas.4:8, it is the <u>opposite of being double-minded</u> – "Purify your hearts, you double-minded." If we say we have the mind of Christ, but have not died to sin and the world, we are double-minded (Rom.6:11-14; Gal.6:14). In Jas.1:8, double-mindedness is mixing faith with doubt, i.e. not pure faith, and not out of a pure heart (2 Tim.2:22).

Any sin that we entertain in our lives, in thought, word or action defiles our purity. Horror movies, violent computer games, hard-rock music and vulgar pornography websites, etc. are from the pit of Hell, designed by Satan to corrupt us. More subtle are the counterfeits that may seem good on the surface, but are actually deadly, defiling our minds and hearts with new-age philosophy and turning us from God to follow occult-based methods of healing and exercise. May God open our eyes and bring us to our knees in repentance, for cleansing and restoration to the purity of Christ, to become the spotless Bride that Jesus died for.

I pray you will take these words seriously. As children of light, rescued from the kingdom of darkness, let us walk in the Light, led by the Holy Spirit. Let us resist the temptation of the world, the flesh and the devil, through the power of God's Spirit and His Word, following His paths of purity. See Eph.4:21-32.

97
HANDLE WITH CARE

*L*abels on clothing don't just tell us what materials are in the fabric. They also give us instructions on how to care for the garment. The level of care depends on the fabric. You can't treat a silk blouse the same as you would a pair of jeans. Just as true is the fact that the fabric of our lives differs greatly from person to person. The knocks and bumps that make some people strong and resilient, in others often tear at the fiber of their being, and their once-vibrant personalities become dull and colorless. We all realize that specific instructions on the care of a child do not come with the baby. Even if they did, many would not read the instructions, let alone follow them. So, at the hands of less than perfect parents, (or grand-parents, etc.), many a fabric of life is marred, badly scarred or ruined, beyond feasible redemption.

An old quote says: "<u>Life is fragile – Handle with prayer</u>." This is so true in the parent-child world, and often makes the difference between disaster and delight. But it also stands true for all of our lives. How many wrong decisions and searing disappointments we could avoid by seeking God's face, and the guidance of the Holy Spirit in every area of our lives. God is, after all, our Father, and wants to protect us from harm, and from our own willful ways, as well as from the snares of this world and the evil one! (Psa.91 reminds us to stay in our place of safety in Him.)

Not long ago, as I was writing this book, using the Microsoft WORD program, I was signing off the computer when some words scrolling across the bottom of the screen caught my eye. It was the normal document-closing jargon, but it hit me with a new meaning. It read: "WORD is saving The Fabric of Life." Ignoring the fact that it didn't say <u>The</u> WORD, (after all, for the believer, there is only one WORD), I excitedly decided to bring this truth in to the book at some point. So, voila!

I don't think we can be reminded too often that God has given us His Word as our life-line (Psa.119:93). It is our guide, the light for our path, our mind-sweeper, instruction book, protection from sin, our key to success (Psa.119:35, 105; Eph.5:26; 2 Tim.3:16; Psa.119:11; Josh.1:8, Psa.1:2-3) and so much more. It is our spiritual nourishment, our delight, our strength, our hope and our help. It brings peace and joy to our innermost being, because it is from God's heart of love to our seeking hearts. His Word is truth, revealed to us and enlightened by the Holy Spirit. By the Word we are warned and corrected. Finally, through the Word of God "have been given to us exceedingly great and precious promises, that through these you may be partakers of the divine nature, having escaped the corruption that is in the world through lust." (2 Pet.1:4) Truly this precious Word of Life saves (redeems, restores and protects) the fabric of our lives! AMEN!!

98
"IF YOU LOVE ME"

*Y*ou may have noticed that I have emphasized the fact that the events of our lives, and even the lives of our ancestors (through our genes) have ingrained effects on the fabric of our life, either for good or for bad. If you are numbered among the few who have a good inheritance, a happy childhood with loving parents and freedom from generational disease and curses, thank God for this every day. But often, without realizing it, some of us carry things in our memory that, be they real or imagined, have left us feeling insecure and inferior/inadequate. If you have been around people at all, you have probably observed some of the tell-tale signs of this. Here are a few: a constant need for affirmation, and approval; always looking for compliments; doing and saying things that make you look good; making demeaning remarks to people; outbursts of anger; holding grudges; taking offence when no offence is intended; causing offence by being condescending; breaking off relationships if someone doesn't live up to your expectations; trying to change/control people; being judgmental, critical and self-righteous; needing to have the last word, to voice your opinion, even if it might hurt others, et al.

The incongruity here is that you might often aver your great love for Jesus, Who said, "If you love me, keep my commandments."

What <u>are</u> Jesus' commandments? He summed them up in three words: "Love one another" (i.e. love those in the body of Christ). The longer version is found in Matt., chapters 5 through 7. Again I will just refer to a few you may need to revisit: "***<u>love</u>*** <u>your enemies</u>, ***<u>bless</u>*** <u>those who curse you</u>, ***<u>do</u>*** ***<u>good to</u>*** <u>those who hate you</u>, and ***<u>pray for</u>*** <u>those who spite-fully use you</u>". "<u>Do not do your charitable deeds before men</u>, to be seen by them." "<u>If you do not</u> ***<u>forgive</u>***<u>, neither will your</u> <u>Father forgive</u>" (you). "***<u>Judge not.</u>***"

In conjunction with Jesus' new commandment to His followers, it might be a good time to check out the characteristics of <u>real</u> love in 1 Cor.13, to see if <u>your</u> love measures up. To paraphrase: ***Love always shows patience and kindness; it's never envious at others' successes; it doesn't exalt you above others in your mind or think badly of others; it isn't ever rude or selfish, and it doesn't take offence; it doesn't quit, but just keeps loving. Without this kind of unconditional love, all your talk is meaningless, and all your works are just a loud, raucous noise in the ears of God.*** Maybe that's why He can't hear your prayers?

> "Beloved, <u>let us love one another</u>, for love is of God: and everyone who loves is born of God and loves God. He who does not love does not know God, for God is love. Beloved, if God so loved us, we also ought to love one another" (1 John 4:7-8, 11).

99
GET ON BOARD

A couple of decades ago, I was part of a Bible Study based on Henry Blackaby's book "Experiencing God". I remember well one of his repeated sayings, that we needed to find out what God is doing, and join Him in it. Oddly enough I can't recall discovering <u>how</u> to do that, let alone doing it. Today I visited his website, and noticed he has another book, "Experiencing the Spirit: The Power of Pentecost Every Day". Now that got my attention! You may have noticed over the past several months there's an astounding plethora of preaching and writing about the work of the Holy Spirit, about spiritual warfare, about miracles, signs and wonders happening today all over the world. More and more preachers I have listened to over the years are realizing that their messages must no longer be "with persuasive words of human wisdom, but in demonstration of the Spirit and of power" (1 Cor.2:4).

Yet there are still those who resist the Holy Spirit. Stephen's words to the religious teachers of Israel are so apropos today: "<u>You always resist the Holy Spirit; as your fathers did, so do you</u>". God <u>so</u> wants to work in His church, (believers in the body of Christ) to make it a mighty powerhouse against the gates of Hell, and to confirm His message of Salvation with signs and wonders. Instead of the Holy Spirit at work in lives to cleanse, restore and empower, what we see so often is self-righteous dead works; lip service rather than worship in

Spirit and truth; and manifestation of the works of the flesh instead of the Spirit's fruit (Gal.5:19-22).

If the fire of the Holy Spirit is quenched (1 Thes.5:19), our love grows cold, and our witness becomes lifeless. Let us heed the words of Jesus to the church at Ephesus in Rev.2:5: "<u>Remember</u> from where you have fallen; <u>repent</u> and do the first works, or I will come to you quickly and remove your lampstand from its place—unless you repent". What <u>were</u> the first works? They were the works recorded in the Book of Acts (not the works of the apostles, but of the Holy Spirit in His people). See John 14:12.

It is time to awake out of our slumber, and see what God is doing in His church today, as people allow the Holy Spirit to do what He wants to do. This is not the hour for us to stand on the sidelines and watch the church march on without us because God is working in ways that don't fit our paradigm. It's past <u>time to shift</u> <u>our paradigm</u>. Pastors and parishioners alike, I challenge you:

- Get on your knees and repent of resisting the Holy Spirit;
- Get back to the Word. Read what God says about His Spirit;
- Get your thinking revised and renewed by the truth;
- Get baptised and empowered with the Holy Spirit;
- Get on board with the new thing God is doing today! See Joel 2:28-29.

100
RECAPITULATION

*I*n this final chapter, I would like to leave a few thoughts with you that I have written down over the past year, to remind you of some of the main truths that have come through in these stories from my life. I hope it will be the Biblical truths you remember rather than the strange but true tales. The following quips or quotes are in no particular order, but as you ponder them, I trust that you can identify with some, and will have gained a fuller understanding of others. (Please bear with a bit of alliteration.)

I am fearfully and wonderfully made in His image.

He wove me together in my mother's womb.

God knows and cares about every detail of my life.

Jesus' blood cleanses me from all sin!

He forgives all my iniquities and heals all my diseases.

"If you don't let your past die, it won't let you live."- Perry Moore

I can face the future freed from the past.

I have shed the shackles of shame. I am walking in His light!

I am free from fear's fetters; I live in God's perfect love.

He brought me from victimization to victory.

I am not a slave; I claim all the rights of sonship in Father's house.

I have a new identity in Christ, and a new DNA.

<u>Whose</u> I am is more important than <u>who</u> I am.

I am reclaiming what the enemy has stolen from me. YEAH!

I am enjoying Kingdom blessings now – His kingdom is in me!

I travel unafraid through enemy territory – he can't touch me!

God takes me where I am, but doesn't leave me there.

The triune God (Father, Son and Holy Spirit) is always with me.

Greater is the One in me than the one in the world.

Jesus has given me authority over the enemy, in His name!

God has given me everything I need for life and godliness!

I can forgive myself and others because God has forgiven me.

I am dead to sin and the world, and they are dead to me.

I have been made perfect before God, by Christ's righteousness.

God resists the proud but gives grace to the humble.

I choose to listen to the voice of God, not other voices.

I have a great Treasure in the earthen vessel that is my body.

I rise as on eagle wings. I run and am not weary. God is my might.

His grace is greater than my disgrace – so amazing!

If God is in control, my life will never be out of control!

God's Word is a lamp to my feet, and a light on my path.

As I yield to the Holy Spirit, He shows me His perfect will.

God wants me to be pure, not popular.

I pray for the peace and salvation of Israel.

In the New Covenant I inherit the blessing of Abraham!

His ways are higher, and His thoughts greater than mine.

Before I call, He answers! Before I speak, He hears!

ALL THIS, AND HEAVEN TOO!!! WHAT ABUNDANT LIFE!!!